MAYER SMITH

Undercover CEO

First edition

This book was professionally typeset on Reedsy.
Find out more at reedsy.com

Contents

One

The CEO's Dilemma

Ethan Sinclair sat in his office, the floor-to-ceiling windows behind him offering a breathtaking view of the San Francisco skyline. The world outside was bathed in the golden glow of the late afternoon sun, but inside his office, the air was thick with tension. His fingers drummed restlessly against the smooth mahogany desk as he stared at the open laptop screen before him. The emails kept piling up, each one more infuriating than the last.

Sir, employees in the customer service department have filed multiple complaints about overwork and mistreatment…

There are reports that TitanTech's lower-level employees have been facing pay cuts while executives receive bonuses…

Mr. Sinclair, I urge you to address the growing unrest among staff before it becomes a PR disaster…

The words blurred together in his mind, but the message was clear—something was wrong within the company he had built from the ground up.

TitanTech was supposed to be different. When Ethan founded the company over a decade ago, he had promised himself that it wouldn't become another soulless corporate machine that valued profits over people. But now, sitting in his sleek, minimalist office, a place that felt more like a throne room than a workspace, he couldn't ignore the growing sense that his empire had slipped through his fingers.

He leaned back in his chair, rubbing his temples. The reports had been coming in for weeks—anonymous complaints, whispers of employees being pushed to their limits, and rumors of a toxic workplace culture. At first, he had dismissed them. He trusted his executives to handle day-to-day operations while he focused on expansion, acquisitions, and innovation. But trust was proving to be a dangerous thing.

A sharp knock at the door snapped him out of his thoughts.

"Come in," he called, straightening in his seat.

The door opened, and Olivia Carter, his long-time assistant, stepped inside. Dressed in her usual sharp blazer and pencil skirt, she carried an iPad in one hand and a knowing expression on her face.

"You saw the latest reports?" she asked, shutting the door behind her.

Ethan let out a dry chuckle. "Hard to miss. Seems like everyone but me knows what's happening in my own company."

Olivia arched a brow. "You've been too busy playing king to notice what's happening in the kingdom."

Ethan shot her a look, but she was one of the few people who could speak to him like that without consequences.

He exhaled and gestured toward the screen. "Tell me straight, Olivia. How bad is it?"

She sighed and took a seat across from him. "Bad. Morale is at an all-time low. Employees feel disposable. Your name is a ghost in these halls, Ethan. Half of them don't even believe you exist anymore."

That stung. He prided himself on being a leader who wasn't just about the bottom line. But when was the last time he had walked the floors of his own company? Spoke to an employee who wasn't a senior executive? He couldn't remember.

"I've read the reports," he said. "But I need to see it for myself."

Olivia tilted her head. "What are you saying?"

"I'm saying," he said, leaning forward, "that I need to go undercover."

She blinked. "You want to—what? Pretend to be one of your employees?"

"Not just any employee. A janitor."

Olivia burst out laughing, but when she saw the seriousness in his expression, the laughter faded. "Oh, you're not joking."

"Not even a little."

She studied him carefully. "This is insane, Ethan. Do you know how ridiculous you'll look if anyone finds out?"

"That's why no one can find out," he said. "Think about it, Olivia. If I walk in as the CEO, people will put on a show. But if I go in as a nobody, I'll get the truth."

She crossed her arms, clearly skeptical. "And you think you can pull this off? You—who probably haven't cleaned a spill in your life—are going to blend in with the janitorial staff?"

"I'll figure it out."

She sighed. "You're serious about this."

"As serious as I was when I built this company."

Olivia shook her head but tapped a few things on her iPad. "Fine. But you'll need a fake identity, documents, background checks—"

"Handle it."

"You're really going to make me do this, aren't you?"

"Wouldn't be the first time you've helped me with something crazy."

She let out a defeated groan. "Alright, but if this backfires, I'm moving to Europe and pretending I never knew you."

"Deal."

Ethan felt the faintest flicker of excitement. It had been a long time since he had been in the trenches, since he had seen the company through the eyes of those who made it run. He would get to the bottom of this.

Or die mopping floors trying.

Two

A New Identity

Ethan Sinclair stood in front of the full-length mirror in his penthouse, staring at the stranger looking back at him.

Gone was the impeccably tailored three-piece suit that had become his second skin. In its place was a pair of faded jeans, a plain gray t-shirt that had seen better days, and a worn-out hoodie Olivia had found at a thrift store. His neatly groomed stubble had grown into an uneven scruff, and his normally sleek, combed-back hair was now tousled into an unruly mess. He looked… unrecognizable.

Perfect.

He ran a hand through his hair, feeling the unfamiliarity of it all. It had been years since he'd dressed like this—since he'd been anything other than Ethan Sinclair, billionaire CEO of TitanTech. Now, for the first time in over a decade, he would be just another worker.

No, not even a worker. A janitor.

His lips twisted into a wry smirk. If anyone on the TitanTech board found out about this plan, they'd think he had lost his mind. Maybe he had. But there was no turning back now.

A sharp knock at the door pulled him from his thoughts.

"It's open," he called.

The door swung open, and Olivia walked in, holding a manila folder and a plastic ID badge. She took one look at him and let out a short, amused huff. "Well, you certainly don't look like a billionaire anymore."

"Good," he said, reaching for the ID.

She handed it over. "Meet Eli Carter. Thirty-two. No college degree. Previous experience in maintenance jobs, but nothing solid. Background checks all clear—because, well, I made them clear." She shot him a pointed look. "You now officially exist."

Ethan examined the ID badge in his hand. Eli Carter, Janitorial Staff. The TitanTech logo was stamped in the corner, and the picture was one Olivia had taken earlier—his disheveled, rugged new persona captured perfectly.

"Nice work," he said.

"I'm not done." She placed the manila folder on the table. "This has everything you need—your employee handbook, work schedule, locker number, and a list of janitorial duties." She smirked. "You should probably read that last one. Something tells me you don't know the first thing about mopping floors."

Ethan rolled his eyes. "How hard can it be?"

"Famous last words." She crossed her arms, expression turning serious. "Are you absolutely sure about this, Ethan? Once you step into that building as Eli Carter, you're just another worker. No special treatment, no easy way out."

"That's the point," he said.

She studied him for a long moment before nodding. "Then you need to remember a few things. One, don't act like you own the place. Two, don't get caught slipping up. And three, for the love of God, stay out of the executive floors. If anyone up there sees you, this whole thing falls apart."

"Noted."

Olivia exhaled. "Alright. You start tomorrow. Night shift. 9 PM sharp."

Ethan lifted a brow. "Night shift?"

She smirked. "Welcome to the real world, boss."

The building looked different from the outside.

Ethan had walked through the front doors of TitanTech a thousand times before, but never like this. Never through the employee entrance. Never with an ID badge that didn't open the high-security floors. Never with a uniform that smelled faintly of bleach and industrial soap.

The weight of the janitorial uniform—navy-blue coveralls, scuffed steel-toe boots—felt strange on his body. He had spent his career designing cutting-edge technology, negotiating billion-dollar deals, and shaping the future of artificial intelligence. Now, he was about to spend the night scrubbing toilets.

A bitter chuckle escaped him as he stepped inside.

The moment he entered, he felt the shift. No more private elevators, no more nods of recognition from high-ranking executives. He was invisible here, just another face in the sea of workers.

A bored-looking woman sat behind the security desk, scrolling through her phone. When she finally glanced up, she barely spared him a second look.

"Name?" she asked flatly.

"Eli Carter," he said, the words feeling foreign on his tongue.

She typed something into the system, then handed him a

keycard. "Locker 107. Get changed. Your supervisor is waiting on floor seven."

No welcome to TitanTech. No polite nod. Nothing.

He had built this empire, and yet, here, he was nothing more than a replaceable cog in the machine.

Ethan moved down the hallway, passing rows of lockers and exhausted-looking employees. Some chatted quietly, others kept to themselves. No one paid him any attention.

Once he reached his locker, he changed into his work uniform and stuffed his personal clothes inside. As he did, he overheard two men talking a few feet away.

"You hear about those layoffs?" one muttered.

"Yeah," the other grumbled. "HR's calling it 'budget adjustments,' but we all know what that means. They cut a bunch of IT guys last week. Who's next? Janitorial?"

The first man scoffed. "Please. You think they care about us? The higher-ups don't even know we exist."

Ethan clenched his jaw.

He shut the locker, swiped his keycard for the janitorial storage room, and grabbed a mop and cleaning cart. The handle felt foreign in his grip, and he had to remind himself not to hold it like a weapon.

Alright, he thought. Let's do this.

The moment he stepped onto the seventh floor, the reality of his decision hit him like a freight train.

His supervisor, a burly man with a gut that strained against his uniform, barely looked up from his clipboard. "You the new guy?"

"Yeah," Ethan said. "Eli."

"Great. Listen up, Eli. We don't do slow here. You clean, you move. No standing around, no wasting time. Got it?"

"Got it."

The man—his name tag read Franklin—grunted. "Bathrooms first. And don't half-ass it."

Ethan grabbed his cart and wheeled it toward the restroom, ignoring the sinking feeling in his gut.

He had spent years reviewing financial reports, analyzing market trends, and making high-level strategic decisions. Now, he was standing in front of a restroom stall, holding a toilet brush.

The stench of industrial cleaner burned his nose.

For the first time in a long time, doubt crept in.

Could he really do this? Could he truly step down from the throne and live like an ordinary worker?

As he scrubbed the porcelain, the voices of the employees from the locker room echoed in his mind.

"The higher-ups don't even know we exist."

Maybe it was time to change that.

Ethan straightened, gripping the brush tighter.

He had come here for a reason. And he wouldn't leave until he found the truth.

Three

The Harsh Reality

E than's hands ached. His back throbbed. His knees felt like they had been hammered into the ground.

And it had only been three hours.

He had never in his life worked like this. Never scrubbed grime off of bathroom tiles, never hauled overflowing trash bags that smelled like something had died inside them, never wiped down conference room tables while employees walked past without sparing him so much as a glance.

For the first time, Ethan Sinclair—the billionaire tech mogul, the genius behind TitanTech, the man whose ideas had changed the world—was invisible.

And it stung.

As he pushed his janitorial cart down the hall, he caught his reflection in the glass wall of a meeting room. His uniform was already wrinkled from sweat, the blue fabric clinging uncomfortably to his skin. A stray lock of hair stuck to his forehead. He looked nothing like the man who had sat in the executive chair of this very building less than twenty-four hours ago.

He looked… small.

Ethan clenched his jaw and kept walking.

This was what he had signed up for.

He needed to see the truth.

Floor seven was quieter now. The day shift had gone home, leaving behind the night crew—janitors, security guards, a few IT workers fixing server issues.

It was the side of TitanTech most never saw.

As Ethan turned a corner, he spotted a group of employees chatting near the break room. They were customer service reps, based on their badges. He had barely noticed them before, but now, standing in his janitor's uniform, he saw them differently.

Two men in button-down shirts leaned against the counter, laughing over coffee. A woman in a maroon sweater scrolled through her phone, exhaustion written all over her face. A younger guy, barely out of his twenties, rubbed his temples while staring at his laptop screen.

Then, there was the manager.

Ethan recognized him immediately—Ryan Calloway.

He had seen Ryan's name in emails before. Heard of him in board meetings. He was a mid-level manager in customer service, someone the executives called "efficient" but whose employees seemed to hate.

Ryan stood in the center of the group, holding a disposable coffee cup like it was a scepter. He was tall, blond, and had the smug confidence of a man who knew he had power over everyone around him.

And Ethan could already tell—he wasn't the type to wield that power kindly.

As Ethan wheeled his cart past them, Ryan's voice cut through the air.

"Hey, janitor," he called, not even looking at him.

Ethan slowed but didn't respond.

Ryan snapped his fingers. "You. Mop guy. Coffee spill, ten feet that way."

Ethan turned. There was a dark stain near the counter. Probably someone had spilled earlier.

He gritted his teeth and forced himself to nod. "Got it."

Ryan didn't say thank you.

Didn't even acknowledge him after that.

Ethan grabbed the mop and started cleaning, listening as the conversation around him continued.

"—three back-to-back calls with customers cursing me out," one of the customer service reps groaned. "And for what? Because their app crashed? Like I designed the damn thing?"

"Try dealing with the Titan One warranty complaints," another said bitterly. "People act like we're hoarding their refunds personally."

Ryan took a slow sip of his coffee. "That's because they don't understand how business works. Customers whine. Employees whine. It's just noise. You have to tune it out."

The young guy at the laptop frowned. "Easy for you to say. You're not the one answering fifty calls a night."

Ryan's smirk widened. "That's why I became a manager. So I don't have to."

A few forced chuckles.

Ethan kept mopping.

He should have been furious. Should have wanted to slam Ryan's entitled face into the coffee-stained floor. But instead, a slow realization crept over him.

This was what TitanTech had become.

His company.

His employees.

And he had let it happen.

Later, when the break room conversation faded and the employees went back to work, Ethan pushed his cart down to the janitorial supply closet.

As he approached, he saw an older man standing outside, wiping his hands on a rag. He had gray hair, a weathered face, and the kind of tired eyes that had seen too much.

The man glanced at Ethan's uniform, then at his face. "You the new guy?"

"Eli," Ethan said, remembering his cover.

"Jim," the man replied. "Welcome to the bottom of the ladder."

Ethan let out a dry chuckle. "Appreciate it."

Jim opened the supply closet, revealing shelves of cleaning supplies, industrial-sized detergent, and spare mops. He grabbed a clipboard from the wall. "So, you survive your first few hours?"

"Just barely."

Jim grinned. "Yeah, you look like you're regretting life choices. That's normal."

Ethan leaned against the cart. "How long you been working here?"

"Twenty years."

Ethan's eyebrows lifted. "Twenty?"

Jim nodded. "Started when TitanTech was still a startup. Back when this place actually gave a damn about its workers." He let out a chuckle, but there was no humor in it. "Now? We're ghosts. No one notices us unless they need something cleaned up."

Ethan thought back to Ryan snapping his fingers at him like he was a dog.

Jim shook his head. "But you learn to live with it. Just keep your head down, do the job, and don't make trouble."

Ethan frowned. "That's it?"

Jim shrugged. "What else is there?"

Ethan had no answer.

Jim clapped him on the shoulder. "Come on. I'll show you how to clean the executive lounge without getting your ass fired."

As Ethan followed Jim down the hall, they passed another group of employees chatting near the vending machines.

One of them—a woman with dark curls and a TitanTech hoodie—spoke up.

"Did you hear?" she said. "Apparently, Sinclair's back in town."

Ethan's stomach tensed.

Another worker, a guy in a baseball cap, scoffed. "Please. That guy's a ghost. We'll never see him."

"Yeah, well, maybe he should show up for once," the woman muttered. "Because this company is turning to crap, and he's the one letting it happen."

Ethan gripped the handle of his cart tighter.

Jim nudged him. "See? Ghosts. Told you."

Ethan forced out a chuckle, but inside, his mind was racing.

His name was spoken like a curse.

His company—his legacy—was becoming something he didn't

even recognize.

And for the first time in years, he felt something he hadn't felt in a long time.

Not anger. Not frustration.

Shame.

Real, deep, gut-wrenching shame.

He had built TitanTech to be different.

Now, it was just another soulless machine.

And unless he did something about it, it would crush the very people who kept it running.

Ethan exhaled slowly.

This wasn't just about going undercover anymore.

It was about fixing what he had broken.

And he was just getting started.

Firecracker

The screech of the industrial vacuum filled the air as Ethan wheeled his janitorial cart down the narrow hallway of TitanTech's seventh floor. His hands ached from gripping the mop for hours, and the stiff uniform clung uncomfortably to his back, damp with sweat. He had expected hard work. What he hadn't expected was the overwhelming nothingness—the way people passed by him like he didn't exist, how his presence barely registered to anyone in the building.

No nods. No greetings.

Just another shadow in the underbelly of his own empire.

He pushed through the exhaustion and turned the corner toward the customer service department. This was where the real complaints were coming from—the reports of overworked employees, impossible quotas, and a management team that seemed to thrive on intimidation. If he was going to get a true sense of what was happening, this was the place to do it.

He had barely taken two steps inside the open-plan office when he heard a voice cut through the dull hum of keyboards and murmured phone calls.

A sharp, irritated, furious voice.

"You're telling me I have to handle seventy calls tonight because Jason called out? Are you serious?"

Ethan turned his head toward the sound, curiosity piqued.

The voice belonged to a woman—a young Latina with dark, wavy hair pulled into a messy ponytail. She stood in the middle of the department, hands on her hips, staring down the manager at the front desk.

He recognized her immediately.

Lena Ramirez.

She had been mentioned in the reports—one of the hardest-working employees in customer service, someone who routinely stayed late to help struggling coworkers, the type of worker who should have been promoted long ago but somehow never was.

And she was furious.

Ryan Calloway, the smug manager Ethan had already pegged as a problem, leaned back in his chair with a lazy smirk. "That's how shift coverage works, Ramirez. Someone calls out, someone else picks up the slack."

Lena let out a bitter laugh. "Seventy calls, Ryan? That's not 'picking up slack'—that's a death sentence. And I guarantee you if it were one of your favorites, you'd be shifting their workload onto the rest of us instead."

Ryan's smirk faltered, but he recovered quickly. "You're on thin ice, Ramirez."

"So are you," she shot back.

Ethan barely managed to suppress a chuckle.

Lena was fire.

She was one of the few employees here who wasn't afraid to push back, to speak her mind even when she had nothing to gain from it. It was a rare thing in corporate environments, where fear of unemployment kept most people silent.

Ryan's nostrils flared. "Either take the calls or go home. Your choice."

Lena clenched her jaw, the muscles in her neck tightening. For a moment, Ethan thought she might actually deck him.

Instead, she let out a slow breath, her shoulders dropping

slightly. "Fine," she said through gritted teeth. "But don't expect me to stay quiet forever."

Ryan didn't bother responding. He turned away, dismissing her like she wasn't worth his time.

Lena muttered something under her breath before storming toward the break room.

Ethan hesitated only for a second before following.

The break room was empty except for Lena, who was aggressively shoving a dollar bill into the vending machine.

She pressed the button for a soda, and nothing happened.

She pressed it again.

Still nothing.

With a growl of frustration, she smacked the side of the machine.

"You planning to fight it, or should I call for backup?" Ethan said, leaning casually against the doorway.

Lena spun around, eyes narrowing. "You got a smart mouth for a janitor."

He shrugged. "I have my moments."

Her gaze swept over him briefly before she turned back to the vending machine. "Damn thing ate my dollar."

Ethan stepped forward, tapping the machine lightly on the side. It whirred, and a can of soda clunked into the slot below.

Lena blinked. "What the hell?"

"Little trick I learned," he said. "You gotta hit it in the right spot."

She eyed him suspiciously before grabbing the soda. "Thanks, I guess."

"Rough night?"

Lena scoffed. "What gave it away? The fact that my manager is a walking piece of human garbage, or the fact that I now have to take seventy calls in a single shift?"

"Both, probably."

She popped the tab on the soda and took a long sip. "I don't get it. This company makes billions. They could hire more people, fix the workload, make this place actually bearable. But instead, they cut corners, overwork us, and expect us to just deal with it."

Ethan's grip on his cart tightened.

She's not wrong.

But he kept his face neutral. "And you stick around why?"

Lena let out a dry chuckle. "Because I have bills, a sick mom, and a degree that means nothing without experience. So, yeah. I stick around." She exhaled sharply and looked at him again. "You new?"

"Yeah. First shift."

She smirked. "Let me guess. You're already regretting it."

He chuckled. "Something like that."

Lena tilted her head slightly, studying him like she was trying to figure something out. "You don't talk like a janitor."

Ethan raised a brow. "How does a janitor talk?"

She shrugged. "I don't know. Just… different."

He could feel her suspicion, the way her eyes flickered with curiosity. He needed to be careful. If anyone figured out who he really was, this whole thing would collapse.

So he just smiled. "Guess I'm full of surprises."

Lena took another sip of her soda, still watching him. Then, with a sigh, she shook her head. "Well, Eli, word of advice—don't get comfortable here. This place chews people up and spits them out. No one gives a damn about the little guys."

Ethan leaned against the counter, folding his arms. "Maybe that needs to change."

Lena let out a bitter laugh. "Good luck with that."

Then, before he could respond, she turned and walked back to her desk, shoulders squared, determination burning in her stride.

Ethan stayed behind, staring after her.

She was wrong about one thing.

Someone cared about the little guys.

And for the first time, he realized—he wasn't just here to observe.

He was here to fix this.

And maybe, just maybe, Lena Ramirez was going to be the key to doing it.

Five

The Bond Begins

Ethan leaned against the janitorial cart, pretending to wipe down the already clean counter in the break room. His body ached from hours of scrubbing floors and hauling garbage, but his mind was racing.

Lena Ramirez.

She wasn't just another overworked employee. She was the kind of person who refused to be crushed under the weight of corporate indifference. She fought back. She cared.

And she absolutely despised people like him.

That part stung more than he expected.

He had spent years believing he was different from the other billionaires—the ones who exploited, cut corners, and lived in a world too far removed from reality. But from the way Lena talked about TitanTech, about him, he realized that somewhere along the way, he had become exactly the kind of CEO she loathed.

And the worst part?

He deserved it.

As he mulled over this uncomfortable truth, he heard footsteps approaching.

Lena.

She had barely taken a break since her argument with Ryan Calloway, and from the dark circles under her eyes, she wasn't planning on taking one anytime soon. She moved with a clipped, frustrated energy, her hands clenched at her sides as she walked toward the vending machine again.

Ethan watched as she dug into her pocket and pulled out a handful of crumpled dollar bills, feeding one into the slot. The machine whirred, then spit the bill back out.

She exhaled sharply, smoothing it against her thigh before trying again.

Same result.

"Seriously?" she muttered, rubbing her temples.

"Let me guess," Ethan said from behind her. "It stole your money again?"

Lena turned, one brow arched. "What, do you moonlight as a vending machine whisperer?"

He smirked. "I like to think of it as strategic percussive maintenance."

She blinked. "You mean kicking it?"

"Exactly."

She huffed but stepped aside, folding her arms as he tapped the machine in a specific spot. With a low hum, the machine accepted the bill.

Lena's lips parted slightly, as if she was reluctant to be impressed. "Alright, janitor. I'll admit—that's a useful skill."

He shrugged. "I have my moments."

She pressed the button for a candy bar, then turned to him. "So, how's your first night in the trenches?"

Ethan glanced down at his mop, the scent of industrial cleaner still sharp in his nose. "About as glamorous as you'd expect."

Lena let out a short laugh, but there was a tired edge to it. "Yeah, well, welcome to the side of TitanTech that no one cares about."

He hesitated, then asked, "Has it always been like this?"

She frowned slightly, peeling back the wrapper of her candy bar. "No. It used to be better. Before all the cutbacks, before management started treating us like machines instead of people."

Ethan felt a lump form in his throat.

She's talking about your decisions. The ones you never even realized were hurting them.

"And now?" he asked.

Lena took a bite, chewing slowly before answering. "Now, it's all about numbers. Call quotas, efficiency ratings, script adherence. You're not allowed to help people anymore. You just read the script and move to the next caller. The second you fall behind, you're disposable."

Ethan absorbed her words, the weight of them settling heavily in his chest.

"So why stay?" he asked.

She shot him a look. "Do I look like someone with options?"

He frowned. "You could get another job."

She let out a short, humorless laugh. "Yeah, let me just snap my fingers and land a cushy six-figure salary."

"That's not what I meant."

Lena sighed, rubbing a hand over her face. "I have a mom with medical bills that never stop coming. A little sister who still needs my help. I don't get the luxury of walking away just because my boss is a jackass."

Ethan clenched his fists.

How had he not known? How had he been so blind to what was happening inside his own company?

Lena was smart. Capable. She should have been running the customer service department, not barely surviving under its weight.

And yet, here she was—stuck in a system he had allowed to fester.

"That's messed up," he said quietly.

Lena snorted. "Yeah. No kidding."

For a moment, they just stood there, the hum of the vending machine the only sound between them.

Then, to his surprise, Lena tilted her head, studying him with mild curiosity. "You're weird for a janitor."

Ethan raised a brow. "Weird how?"

She shrugged. "Most new guys just keep their heads down and get through the night. You actually talk. And not in that fake 'customer service voice' way. Like you actually give a damn."

He hesitated. He couldn't tell if this was suspicion or just an observation.

"I guess I just don't like seeing people get screwed over," he said honestly.

Lena watched him for a second longer, then nodded. "Well, in that case, welcome to the club."

A small, rare smile ghosted over her lips. It was gone in an instant, but Ethan caught it.

And for the first time that night, he realized something.

He wasn't just here to observe anymore.

Lena Ramirez was the kind of person TitanTech needed to survive—the kind of employee who fought for what was right, even when it cost her.

If he wanted to fix what was broken, he needed to understand workers like her.

And more importantly—he needed her to trust him.

Even if she could never know who he really was.

The night dragged on, and Ethan went back to work, but his mind was no longer focused on just playing his part.

Every interaction he had, every dismissive glance from higher-ups, every whispered complaint he overheard—it all painted a clearer picture of what TitanTech had become.

And it wasn't pretty.

At one point, he saw Lena again, headset on, fingers flying over the keyboard as she handled a particularly angry customer.

Her voice was calm, controlled, even when the person on the other end was clearly shouting.

And then—just for a second—her eyes flicked toward him.

He wasn't sure why.

Maybe she was still sizing him up.

Maybe she was wondering why the janitor cared so much.

Or maybe, just maybe, she saw something in him she hadn't expected.

Either way, Ethan knew one thing for certain.

This undercover mission had just gotten a lot more complicated.

Because now?

He wasn't just watching from the sidelines.

He was in the fight.

And Lena Ramirez was the only ally he had.

Six

A Different Perspective

The hum of the fluorescent lights above buzzed in Ethan's ears as he wiped down yet another fingerprint-smudged glass partition. The hours of his night shift dragged on, but exhaustion took a backseat to something more unsettling—the growing realization of just how broken TitanTech had become.

Every conversation he overheard, every exhausted sigh from an overworked employee, every manager barking orders like their subordinates were machines instead of people—it all added up to a stark truth he couldn't ignore.

TitanTech wasn't just flawed.

It was rotting from the inside.

And no one had the guts to do anything about it.

Except, maybe, Lena Ramirez.

He glanced across the office, where she sat at her desk, headset on, fingers flying over the keyboard as she handled a particularly difficult customer.

"Sir, I understand your frustration," she said in a voice that was calm but firm. "But per TitanTech's policy, your refund request must go through our automated system first before—"

A loud click interrupted her. The customer had hung up.

Lena ripped off her headset and let out a frustrated groan. "Unbelievable," she muttered under her breath.

Ethan turned his attention back to his work, but his ears stayed sharp.

The moment Lena's call ended, another rep sitting next to her leaned over and whispered, "That's the third one today, isn't it?"

Lena pinched the bridge of her nose. "Fourth. And every single one of them asked to speak to a manager, but we don't have managers on call at night because the geniuses upstairs decided it wasn't 'cost-efficient.' So guess who gets yelled at instead?"

Her coworker, a guy with shaggy blond hair and dark circles under his eyes, gave a half-hearted chuckle. "Sounds about right. You're lucky Calloway didn't hear you say that. He'd have your ass for 'insubordination.'"

Lena scoffed. "Let him try."

Ethan smirked. She really doesn't know when to quit, does she?

He should have gone back to his cleaning, kept his head down like Olivia had warned him. But something about Lena's fire, her unwillingness to accept things as they were, kept pulling him in.

She wasn't just surviving TitanTech's toxic environment.

She was fighting it.

And if Ethan was going to fix what was broken, he needed to understand her fight.

So, against his better judgment, he wheeled his janitorial cart a little closer.

"Rough night?" he asked casually as he reached Lena's desk.

Lena looked up, recognizing him instantly. "Wow, janitor guy. You're still standing."

Ethan smirked. "Yeah, well, turns out mopping floors doesn't kill you. Who knew?"

Her coworker chuckled but quickly turned back to his screen

when a new call came in.

Lena exhaled sharply, rubbing her temples. "To answer your question—yeah. Rough night. But that's pretty much every night around here."

Ethan leaned against the cart. "Seems like it shouldn't be."

Lena shot him a sideways glance. "You're weirdly opinionated for someone who just got here."

"I'm observant."

She snorted. "Yeah? And what have you observed so far?"

He gestured around the office. "That people here work their asses off for a company that doesn't appreciate them."

Lena let out a dry laugh. "Wow. You figured that out in one night? Damn. You must be a genius."

Ethan raised a brow. "I mean, I have my moments."

That actually got a smirk out of her. But it was short-lived.

She turned her chair toward him, her expression serious now. "Look, new guy—I get it. You're seeing this place for the first time, and you're realizing how screwed up it is. But here's the thing—you can't fix it. No one can. We're replaceable. All of us."

Ethan felt a flicker of something deep in his chest. Anger? Frustration?

Guilt?

"And you're just… okay with that?" he asked.

Lena scoffed. "Hell no. But what choice do we have?"

She leaned forward slightly, lowering her voice so no managers could overhear.

"You think the higher-ups care about us?" she asked. "We're numbers to them. If I quit tomorrow, they'd have someone else in my seat before I finished packing my desk. No severance, no safety net—just gone."

Ethan's jaw tightened. He wanted to tell her she was wrong.

But she wasn't.

Not entirely.

Because if everything he had seen so far was any indication— TitanTech wasn't the company he thought it was.

And that was his fault.

The office suddenly went quiet as Ryan Calloway strode in, clipboard in hand. His eyes swept the room like a predator surveying his territory.

Ethan immediately stiffened.

He had already decided—he didn't like Ryan. And after seeing how he treated Lena, he liked him even less.

Ryan's gaze landed on her, and his lips curled into an unimpressed smirk. "Ramirez," he said, his voice oily and condescending.

Lena straightened but didn't say anything.

Ryan clicked his pen against his clipboard. "I've been reviewing your efficiency reports. Seems like you're three percent below quota this week."

Lena's jaw clenched. "Three percent? Seriously?"

Ryan shrugged. "Rules are rules. If you don't meet the quota, you don't get your incentive bonus."

Ethan saw the way Lena's fingers curled into fists in her lap.

Three percent? That was barely a margin of error.

"You do realize," Lena said slowly, "that I've had to take double the calls this week because you won't authorize backup coverage, right?"

Ryan smiled. "Not my problem."

Ethan wanted to punch him.

Actually, no.

He wanted to fire him.

But right now, Eli Carter was just a janitor.

So he kept his mouth shut.

Lena, however, wasn't backing down.

"Let me guess," she said bitterly. "If I was one of your favorites, you'd be fudging the numbers to make sure I got my bonus, right?"

Ryan tsked. "Careful, Ramirez. You wouldn't want to sound disgruntled."

Lena opened her mouth to respond, but before she could, Ryan turned and walked away, already moving on to his next victim.

Ethan watched as Lena sat back, exhaling sharply, her hands gripping the arms of her chair.

For the first time since meeting her, he saw something in her expression that wasn't just frustration or anger.

It was defeat.

And something about that made his blood boil.

Lena Ramirez wasn't the kind of person who gave up easily.

But TitanTech was breaking her.

And Ethan Sinclair—whether he deserved it or not—was the only person who could stop it.

As the night shift dragged on, Ethan didn't stop thinking about what had just happened.

He had come here to observe.

To understand.

But now?

Now, it wasn't enough to see the problem.

He needed to fix it.

And he knew exactly where to start.

With the firecracker who refused to stay silent.

With Lena Ramirez.

And whether she realized it or not—

She had just become the most important person in this entire damn company.

Seven

The Office Villain

Ryan Calloway strode into the office at precisely 9:00 p.m. as though he owned the place. His expensive leather shoes clicked against the tile floors, his tailored blazer somehow still crisp after an entire day's wear. He carried a clipboard and a self-satisfied smirk, his sharp blue eyes scanning the room like a hawk searching for prey.

The night shift was in full swing, with customer service reps seated at rows of cubicles, headsets on, fingers flying across keyboards as they fielded call after call. The hum of voices, punctuated by the occasional loud complaint from a particularly irate customer, created a low-level buzz that never seemed to fade. Ethan, still disguised as Eli Carter, pushed his janitorial cart quietly along the edge of the room. He kept his head down, but his ears were sharp, catching every word.

"You're below quota again," Ryan's voice rang out, cutting through the noise like a knife. He stopped at one of the desks and leaned against the partition, his posture relaxed but his tone dripping with condescension. "If you can't meet the numbers by the end of the week, I'll have to find someone who can."

The young man at the desk, barely in his twenties, nodded meekly, his shoulders hunching under the weight of Ryan's gaze. "I'll do my best, sir," he mumbled.

Ryan's smirk widened. "See that you do."

Ethan's grip tightened on the handle of his mop. He had been watching Ryan for days now, observing the way he interacted with his team—or rather, the way he lorded over them. The man's every word, every gesture, radiated a sense of superiority. He seemed to take pleasure in pointing out flaws, in making people squirm under his scrutiny. Ethan knew that this kind of management style wasn't just ineffective; it was toxic. And the more he saw, the more he realized just how deep the rot went.

Ryan continued his rounds, his presence a dark cloud that seemed to suck the energy out of the room wherever he went. He stopped at another desk, this time in front of Lena Ramirez. Ethan's stomach knotted.

"Ramirez," Ryan said, drawing her name out as if he were addressing a child who had just spilled juice on the carpet. "I see you're still struggling with those efficiency metrics."

Lena didn't look up. She kept typing, her tone flat as she replied,

"I'm doing my job, Calloway. That's more than I can say for some people."

A few nearby reps stifled nervous chuckles. Ryan's jaw tightened, and his smirk turned into a thin, unpleasant line. He leaned closer, his voice dropping to a low growl. "Watch yourself, Ramirez. Keep talking like that, and you'll find yourself out the door."

Lena's hands paused for just a moment before resuming their rapid pace on the keyboard. "Noted," she said, her voice edged with defiance.

Ethan couldn't help but admire her bravery. She was surrounded by people who were too scared to speak up, and yet Lena never backed down. But he also knew that Ryan's threats weren't empty. The man seemed to enjoy using his position to intimidate, to push people to their breaking points. Ethan had seen it time and time again over the past few days—Ryan picking a target, chipping away at their confidence until they either quit or broke under the pressure.

Tonight, it was clear that Lena was Ryan's target. And while she might have a tough exterior, Ethan could see the cracks forming. Her jaw was tight, her posture rigid. She was holding it together, but barely.

Ethan forced himself to look away before Ryan noticed him. He moved toward the far corner of the office, pretending to focus on wiping down a countertop. But his mind was racing. He had come here to see the reality of TitanTech from the ground level, and what he was seeing was worse than he had imagined.

Ryan Calloway wasn't just a bad manager. He was a bully. And he was getting away with it because no one above him cared enough to stop it.

Ethan's blood boiled. He had built TitanTech with the intention of creating something better—a company that valued innovation, integrity, and its people. But somewhere along the line, that vision had been twisted. And if Ryan Calloway was any indication, the problem wasn't just a few disgruntled employees. It was systemic.

But Ethan couldn't act on that knowledge—yet. As far as anyone here knew, he was just Eli Carter, a lowly janitor. If he confronted Ryan now, his entire cover would be blown. And if Ryan found out who he really was, he'd likely go into damage control mode, covering his tracks and making it that much harder to root out the deeper issues.

No, Ethan needed to bide his time. He needed to gather more information, more proof of what was happening. Then, when the moment was right, he would act. And when he did, Ryan wouldn't know what hit him.

For now, though, Ethan could only watch. He finished cleaning the countertop and moved on to the next section of the office, his movements methodical, his mind focused. Ryan Calloway was the embodiment of everything wrong with TitanTech, and Ethan wasn't going to let him continue unchecked.

As he worked, Ethan caught glimpses of Lena at her desk. Despite the constant pressure, she was still fighting. Still standing up to Ryan. Still doing her best to support her team, even when it cost her. She was exactly the kind of person TitanTech needed more of. And Ryan was exactly the kind of person it needed less of.

Ethan's jaw tightened as he moved his cart down the aisle, his thoughts swirling. He had come here to see how his employees were treated, but now he understood that it wasn't just about observing. It was about taking action. And sooner or later, Ryan Calloway was going to have to answer for the damage he'd done.

And when that day came, Ethan would be ready.

Eight

Unexpected Chemistry

The cafeteria was quiet that night, except for the hum of the vending machines and the faint murmur of conversation from a distant corner. Ethan stood near the far wall, gripping a mug of lukewarm coffee he'd gotten from the break room. His shoulders ached from hours of pushing the janitorial cart, his hands raw from scrubbing the grout in a bathroom that hadn't been properly cleaned in weeks. But his body wasn't what weighed him down.

It was Lena Ramirez.

Over the past several nights, she had become a fixture in his mind. Not just because of her fire or her fierce work ethic, but because she refused to let the company grind her down. She stood up to Ryan Calloway, rallied her colleagues, and took on workloads that should have been divided among three people—

all without asking for recognition or reward. She did it because it was the right thing to do.

And she despised everything Ethan stood for.

It was ironic, really. The very qualities that drew him to her—her honesty, her courage—were the same ones that would likely turn her away if she ever discovered who he really was.

He took another sip of coffee, staring into the middle distance. Just then, the cafeteria door swung open. Ethan turned his head, and there she was—Lena. She walked in with her usual purposeful stride, carrying a stack of files under one arm and a look of determination that was quickly becoming familiar.

She paused when she spotted him. For a moment, she seemed to debate whether or not to acknowledge him. Then, with a sigh, she crossed the room and sat down at a table nearby. She set the files down and glanced up at him. "You planning to hover there all night, or are you going to sit down?"

Caught off guard, Ethan raised an eyebrow but obliged, taking the seat across from her. "Didn't think you'd notice me over here."

"I notice everyone," she said simply, flipping open a folder. "Part of the job."

He smirked. "Seems like you notice more than most."

She didn't respond right away, scanning a page before closing the folder again. Then she leaned back, folding her arms. "You're a curious one, Eli. Most janitors keep their heads down, do their work, and leave. You… watch people. Why?"

Ethan froze for a second, scrambling for a response that wouldn't reveal too much. "It's just how I am, I guess. I like to understand what's going on around me."

She narrowed her eyes, as if weighing the truth of his answer. "Well, here's what's going on around you," she said, leaning forward. "People are being pushed to their breaking points. I've got coworkers who haven't taken a real day off in months because management keeps saying we're short-staffed. I've got team members who are one bad performance review away from losing their jobs. And I've got a boss who cares more about hitting numbers than about the human beings behind them."

Ethan felt a pang of guilt so sharp it nearly made him wince. She was right. Every word of it. And yet, he couldn't admit that he already knew—or that he was responsible for the very conditions she was describing.

Instead, he nodded slowly. "Sounds rough."

"'Rough' doesn't begin to cover it," she said bitterly. "But it's not just me. It's everyone. People who actually care about the work they do are being driven out. And the ones who stay—well, they're just trying to survive."

Ethan could hear the anger in her voice, but there was something else underneath it—something more vulnerable. She cared deeply about her coworkers, about her job, about the company itself. Even if she wouldn't admit it outright, she wanted TitanTech to be better.

And he did too. He always had. But somewhere along the line, he had lost sight of what that meant.

"I don't know how you do it," he said quietly.

Lena snorted. "What, stay sane in this madhouse?"

He gave a faint smile. "Something like that."

She shrugged. "You just… keep going. You hope that maybe, just maybe, someone upstairs will finally wake up and realize what they're doing. And in the meantime, you lean on the people who haven't given up yet."

Ethan leaned back in his chair, considering her words. He couldn't help but admire her optimism, even if it was laced with bitterness. She still believed that change was possible.

"You seem pretty passionate about this place," he said, testing the waters.

Lena's expression hardened. "Don't mistake passion for desperation. I don't love this company. But I've invested too much of my life into it to just walk away."

The silence that followed felt heavy. Ethan wanted to say something, to assure her that not everyone at the top was blind to the problems she was facing. But he knew he couldn't—not yet. He had to stay in character. He had to keep learning, keep listening.

Lena broke the silence first. "What about you, Eli? What's your story?"

He blinked. "My story?"

"Yeah," she said, gesturing toward him. "You don't seem like someone who grew up dreaming of being a janitor. So what's your deal?"

Ethan hesitated. Olivia had prepared a backstory for him—one that would hold up under scrutiny if anyone asked. But now, under Lena's watchful gaze, it felt thin. Forced.

"I've had a few different jobs over the years," he said carefully. "Mostly maintenance and cleaning. Nothing too exciting."

"Sounds like you're dodging the question," she said, a hint of challenge in her tone.

He raised an eyebrow. "Is this an interrogation?"

Lena smirked. "Just making conversation. If you don't want to share, that's fine."

Ethan took a breath, considering his next move. He couldn't reveal his true identity, but maybe he didn't need to stick to the script either. Maybe he could just be… honest. At least a little.

"I used to be in a different line of work," he said finally. "Something more… corporate. But I got tired of all the red tape. All the fake smiles and empty promises. I wanted something simpler."

Lena's smirk faded. "Huh. Didn't expect that."

"Didn't expect what?"

She shrugged. "You don't talk like a guy who's tired of the corporate world. You talk like someone who still cares about it."

Ethan's chest tightened. She was sharp—too sharp. If he wasn't careful, she'd see right through him. But he couldn't backpedal now. He had to roll with it.

"Maybe I do," he said, his voice steady. "But that doesn't mean I want to be part of it anymore."

Lena studied him for a long moment before nodding. "Fair enough."

For a while, neither of them spoke. The cafeteria felt oddly calm, the hum of the vending machines filling the silence. And though they hadn't said much, Ethan felt like he understood Lena a little better. She wasn't just fighting for herself—she was fighting for everyone around her. And maybe, in some small way, she was starting to see him as more than just the new janitor.

The thought sent a strange warmth through his chest. For the first time in a long time, he felt… connected. To her. To the people here. To something bigger than himself.

It was a dangerous feeling, but one he couldn't ignore.

Ethan stood, gripping his coffee cup. "I should get back to work."

Lena nodded. "Me too."

As he walked away, he could feel her eyes on him. And though he didn't turn back, he couldn't shake the thought that, in that moment, something between them had shifted.

Nine

Cracks in the Facade

The break room's clock ticked faintly, the only sound against the stillness of the late-night shift. Ethan sat at the far table, his mop propped against the wall beside him, a half-empty coffee cup cradled in his hands. He stared at the tabletop, trying to piece together the past few weeks' events.

It wasn't going according to plan.

What had started as a simple undercover mission to observe had become more complicated. Every night, Ethan learned more about the struggles of TitanTech's lower-level employees, their sacrifices, and the invisible weights they carried. The more he saw, the more he wanted to help. But the closer he got to them—especially to Lena Ramirez—the harder it became to maintain his cover.

Lena didn't trust easily. She had good reason not to. Yet, over the past few weeks, she'd started to soften toward him. Not by much, but enough that Ethan could sense it. She'd ask his opinion on small things—like what drink he'd recommend from the vending machine—or complain about Calloway in his presence without immediately brushing him off afterward. It wasn't friendship, exactly. It was more like a hesitant truce. And with each conversation, each shared moment in the quiet hours of the night, he found himself drawn to her resilience, her strength, her unwavering sense of justice.

But that connection made his disguise all the more fragile.

Every now and then, she'd give him a look—a curious, searching glance that made him wonder if she was piecing together the truth. She never said anything outright, but the questions started to come. Simple ones at first: "Where'd you work before this?" "How'd you end up at TitanTech?" "What made you want to clean toilets for a living?" He brushed them off with vague answers, but Lena wasn't the type to let things slide. Her curiosity was relentless, and each deflection only seemed to fuel her suspicion.

Then there were the moments he slipped up.

The night before, he had helped a new hire find the supply room. The young woman had been struggling with the outdated map she'd been given, and without thinking, Ethan rattled off directions as if he'd known the building for years. Lena had overheard and raised an eyebrow.

"Impressive memory," she'd said. Her tone was casual, but her eyes had been sharp.

He had laughed it off, muttering something about "just paying attention," but the way she looked at him afterward made his stomach tighten. She wasn't buying it.

Tonight, things felt even more precarious. The team had been forced to stay late because of a last-minute product update that sent the call volume through the roof. Lena was on her third coffee, her hair in a messy bun, her sleeves rolled up. She worked through the calls with grit and determination, but it was clear she was at her limit. As the night wore on, her temper grew shorter.

At one point, she stormed into the break room where Ethan was wiping down the counters. She slammed her headset onto the table and rubbed her temples.

"This place is going to kill me," she muttered.

Ethan set the rag down. "Rough night?"

Lena glared at him, but it wasn't anger directed at him. It was frustration—raw and unfiltered. "Rough life, more like."

He leaned on the counter. "Anything I can do?"

She gave him a once-over, then sighed. "Unless you can magically make Calloway disappear, no. I'm stuck."

For a moment, neither of them spoke. Then Lena sank into a chair and stared at the floor.

"I keep telling myself I'll leave," she said quietly. "That I'll find something better. But I never do. Because as bad as it is here, at least it's… predictable. I know what I'm up against. Out there? Who knows what kind of mess I'd walk into."

Ethan's chest tightened. He wanted to tell her she deserved better. That TitanTech shouldn't be a place that crushed people's spirits. But how could he say that without revealing who he really was?

"You shouldn't have to put up with this," he said carefully.

Lena let out a bitter laugh. "Yeah? Tell that to the rent, the medical bills, the student loans. Life doesn't give you a choice. You take what you can get."

She looked up at him then, and there it was again—that searching look. "You talk like you know something I don't. Like you've got it all figured out."

He swallowed hard. "I'm just saying… you're worth more than this."

Lena's eyes narrowed, and for a moment, Ethan thought she might press him further. But then she shook her head and stood.

"Thanks for the pep talk, janitor," she said, her tone more tired than sarcastic. She picked up her headset and headed back out, leaving Ethan alone with his thoughts.

He let out a long breath, his mind spinning. He needed to be more careful. Every conversation with Lena felt like walking a tightrope. He couldn't afford another slip-up, not when she was already suspicious.

As the hours stretched on, Ethan stayed in the background, watching, listening. He overheard Ryan Calloway berating one of the newer reps, his voice dripping with scorn. He saw another employee quietly pack up their things and leave early, their face pale and drawn. He noticed how Lena's colleagues glanced her way whenever something went wrong, as if silently asking her to fix it, even when she had nothing left to give.

Ethan realized something in that moment. He wasn't just seeing the cracks in TitanTech's foundation. He was seeing the people who had been holding it together all along.

And Lena Ramirez was at the center of it.

But the more he saw, the more he questioned his role in this charade. How long could he keep up the act before it all came crashing down? Before Lena—and everyone else—found out the truth?

The thought haunted him as he pushed his cart back into the storage room and closed the door behind him. In the quiet of the small, dimly lit space, he leaned against the wall and let out a heavy sigh.

He had come here to understand what was wrong with his company. Now, he understood all too well. And the knowledge sat like a weight on his chest.

The real question was no longer whether he could fix it.

It was whether he could fix it before the cracks in his facade became too big to hide.

Ten

The Turning Point

Ethan's shift began like all the others—long hours scrubbing tile floors, collecting trash from overflowing bins, and mopping the same stretch of hallway for what felt like the hundredth time. But tonight, something felt different. The weight of his own deception hung heavier than usual. The questions Lena had asked earlier in the week still lingered in his mind. Every time she gave him one of her searching looks, he worried that she saw through him. That she'd figure out he wasn't who he claimed to be.

But tonight wasn't just about Lena. Tonight, it was about what Ethan had discovered—and what he was about to do.

He had spent weeks undercover, observing everything from the insipid management practices of Ryan Calloway to the grinding pressure placed on the night shift employees. He knew he couldn't stay on the sidelines any longer. And yet, stepping out from the shadows meant risking everything. His cover, his plan, his reputation—it all hung in the balance.

His opportunity came in the form of an emergency.

The call came down from management just after midnight: a major client's system had gone down, and the customer service team needed to stay late to handle the influx of complaints. Managers were scrambling. The skeleton crew on duty was overwhelmed within minutes, calls flooding in faster than they could be answered. The reps were snapping at each other, frustration bubbling over. Lena, as always, was in the thick of it, taking call after call, her voice calm but her body language tense.

Ethan watched from the edge of the room, pretending to mop the same spot on the floor while listening to the chaos unfold. The managers weren't helping. Calloway was barking orders, pushing people harder, while other supervisors whispered among themselves, trying to figure out who could be blamed if the situation escalated. Not a single person in charge seemed to care about what their employees were going through.

It was exactly the kind of moment Ethan had feared—and exactly the kind of moment he had been waiting for.

When the third tech support rep broke down in tears, mumbling apologies as their headset slipped off, Ethan knew he couldn't wait any longer. This was the breaking point. The company's facade was crumbling right before his eyes.

Lena was holding it together, barely. She hung up one call and immediately answered the next, her voice steady but strained. When Calloway strode past her desk, glowering, she ignored him, her fingers flying over her keyboard as she pulled up another troubleshooting guide.

But then it happened.

The customer on the other end of the line—angry, frustrated, and desperate—demanded to speak to someone higher up. Lena calmly explained that no managers were available at this hour, but the customer wasn't having it. They threatened to escalate the issue to the press, to cancel their account, to go directly to the CEO if necessary. Lena's face remained calm, but her hands trembled slightly as she reached for her water bottle.

Calloway heard the commotion and walked over. "Ramirez," he snapped. "What's going on?"

Lena held up a hand, motioning for him to wait. "I'm trying to resolve the issue," she said, her voice measured. "But they want to speak to a manager."

Calloway scoffed. "We've been through this. No managers on call at night. Handle it."

"I'm trying," Lena said, her jaw tightening. "But they're threatening to escalate. We need someone to step in."

Calloway leaned down, his tone dripping with disdain. "You

think I'm going to waste my time dealing with some irate client in the middle of the night? Do your job, Ramirez."

Lena stared at him, her expression blank but her knuckles white as she gripped the edge of her desk. She said nothing, simply put her headset back on and continued the call.

Ethan watched all of this unfold, his stomach twisting. He couldn't just stand there anymore. Not after everything he'd seen. Not after everything he'd learned about how deeply the company he had built had gone off course.

But what could he do? If he spoke up now, if he intervened, he'd risk blowing his cover. Yet, if he didn't, he would be allowing the very problems he'd come here to understand to continue unchecked.

He glanced down at the mop in his hand, at the uniform that hid his true identity. Then he looked back at Lena. She didn't deserve this. None of them did.

The moment stretched into eternity. The noise of the call center faded into a dull hum, and all Ethan could hear was the pounding of his own heartbeat. He had spent so much time hiding in the shadows, waiting for the perfect moment. But maybe the perfect moment didn't exist. Maybe he had to create it.

Taking a deep breath, Ethan stepped forward. He didn't have a plan, not exactly. He didn't have a script or a strategy. All he knew was that he couldn't stand by anymore.

"Excuse me," he said, his voice cutting through the noise.

Lena looked up first, her eyes widening slightly. Calloway turned slowly, an annoyed expression already forming.

"What do you want, janitor?" Calloway sneered.

Ethan met his gaze, his voice steady despite the storm raging inside him. "It's clear that this situation is beyond what the team can handle on their own. If no managers are available, someone needs to take responsibility."

Calloway's sneer deepened. "And you think that's you?"

Ethan took a step closer. "I think it should be someone who actually cares about fixing the problem instead of blaming their employees."

A hush fell over the immediate area. The reps nearby stopped typing, their eyes darting back and forth between Ethan and Calloway. Lena stared at him, her expression unreadable, but there was something in her eyes—something like surprise, maybe even a flicker of respect.

Calloway's face reddened. "You have no idea what you're talking about. Get back to cleaning floors and stay out of things you don't understand."

Ethan's grip on the mop tightened. He wanted to say more, to confront Calloway outright, but he held back. He couldn't afford to reveal everything. Not yet.

Instead, he turned to Lena. "Do you have a suggestion for how to de-escalate the situation?"

Lena blinked, clearly caught off guard. "I… we could offer a temporary workaround. Something to keep the client satisfied until the day shift can take over."

Ethan nodded. "Then let's try that."

Calloway opened his mouth to protest, but Ethan cut him off. "We're all trying to keep the company running smoothly, aren't we? Let's work together instead of pointing fingers."

The room was silent for a long moment. Then, slowly, Lena nodded. "I'll handle it."

She put her headset back on, her voice calm as she spoke to the client. Ethan stepped back, the tension in his chest easing just a fraction.

Calloway glared at him but said nothing, eventually stomping off toward his office. The other reps gradually returned to their calls, and the chaos began to settle.

Ethan returned to his cart, his hands trembling slightly as he resumed his work. He had walked a fine line, but he had managed to make a difference without completely blowing his cover.

But as the night wore on, he couldn't shake the feeling that he had crossed a line—one that he couldn't uncross. And deep down, he knew that the next time something like this happened, it might not be so easy to keep his true identity hidden.

Eleven

A Test of Character

The soft hum of fluorescent lights flickered above the seventh-floor breakroom. The coffee machine gurgled weakly, half-heartedly dispensing the last few drops of a stale brew into a cracked pot. Ethan stood near the counter, gripping his mop as if it were a lifeline. His cover as Eli Carter was growing harder to maintain, and tonight's events had only made it worse.

Lena Ramirez leaned against the far wall, arms crossed. She wasn't her usual fiery self. Instead, there was a quiet exhaustion about her that made Ethan uneasy. She'd just come off another brutal call, and it showed. The tension in her shoulders, the tightness around her mouth—everything about her radiated frustration.

"I don't get it," she muttered. "How can a company this big be this broken?"

Ethan didn't respond right away. He'd been asking himself the same question for weeks. TitanTech had always been his pride, his legacy. Now it felt like a stranger's creation—a machine that ground down good people like Lena without a second thought.

"It shouldn't be," he said finally.

Lena's eyes narrowed slightly as she looked at him. "What do you mean?"

"I mean, someone at the top must know what's going on," Ethan replied carefully. "It's hard to believe they're completely blind to it."

She gave a bitter laugh. "You think Sinclair cares about us? He's probably sitting in his mansion, sipping hundred-dollar scotch, while the rest of us are drowning."

Ethan's jaw tightened. "Maybe he just doesn't know. Maybe he would care if he did."

Lena snorted. "Yeah, sure. And maybe pigs will fly." She pushed off the wall and grabbed a can of soda from the vending machine. "I've been here long enough to know that people like him don't see us. We're invisible to them. Replaceable."

The words hit Ethan harder than he expected. He had spent years telling himself that TitanTech's success was built on its people. But if Lena's experience was any indication, he had failed to live up to that ideal. And now, as Eli Carter, he was seeing the consequences firsthand.

Lena took a sip of her soda, her eyes studying him over the rim of the can. "You're weird, you know that?"

Ethan blinked. "What?"

"You don't talk like a janitor," she said. "You ask questions like someone who actually gives a damn."

"Maybe I do give a damn," he said, trying to keep his voice light.

"Yeah, well, it's not going to change anything," Lena said flatly. She turned and walked out of the breakroom, leaving Ethan alone with his thoughts.

He let out a slow breath, his mind racing. Lena was sharp, too sharp. Every conversation with her felt like navigating a minefield. He needed to be careful, to keep his story straight, or she'd figure him out.

But as much as her words stung, they also lit a fire inside him. She didn't believe change was possible. She didn't believe that anyone at the top cared. He had to prove her wrong. Not for his own sake, but for hers.

Ethan pushed the mop back into his cart and left the breakroom. The night wasn't over, and there was still work to be done.

As he made his way down the hall, he heard raised voices

coming from the customer service floor. He paused, listening.

"I'm telling you, we can't handle this many calls with the current staff," someone said. "We need more people, or we're going to start losing clients."

Ethan recognized the voice—one of the senior reps. He couldn't see who they were speaking to, but it was clear the situation was escalating.

A second voice responded, sharper and more dismissive. "That's not my problem. Figure it out."

Ryan Calloway.

Ethan's hands curled into fists. Calloway was exactly the kind of manager who thrived in a broken system. He deflected blame, ignored legitimate concerns, and treated his team like disposable parts. And tonight, he was in rare form.

Ethan pushed his cart closer, staying just out of sight. He didn't want to confront Calloway directly—at least not yet. He needed to understand more before he acted.

"You're pushing us too hard," the senior rep said. "People are burning out. We need more resources."

Calloway laughed, a cold, hollow sound. "Resources? This isn't a charity. We all have jobs to do. If you can't handle it, maybe you should find somewhere else to work."

Ethan's jaw tightened. He couldn't believe what he was hearing. Calloway wasn't just a bad manager; he was a liability. If this was how he treated his team in front of others, how much worse was it behind closed doors?

He edged closer, careful to stay out of sight.

Calloway continued. "And if you think whining to HR is going to help, good luck. They report to me, remember? Nothing gets past my desk without my approval."

Ethan's heart pounded. He needed proof—something concrete to expose Calloway's behavior. But how could he get it without blowing his cover?

Then, a sudden crash startled him.

A stack of papers toppled to the floor, and Ethan realized too late that his cart had bumped into the corner of a nearby desk. He froze, hoping no one had noticed.

But Calloway's sharp eyes locked onto him.

"You," he barked. "What the hell are you doing sneaking around?"

Ethan forced a sheepish smile. "Sorry, I was just cleaning the area."

Calloway stormed over, his expression dark. "Clean somewhere else. Now."

Ethan nodded and started to wheel his cart away, but he couldn't shake the feeling that Calloway's eyes were still on him.

As he rounded the corner, he let out a shaky breath. He had been too careless. Calloway's suspicion might fade, but if it didn't, Ethan's entire mission could be jeopardized.

He needed to be smarter. More careful.

And he needed to figure out a way to take Calloway down before more people got hurt.

Twelve

Secrets Unraveling

The building was eerily quiet as Ethan slipped into the locker room after his shift. Most of the employees had gone home, and only the faint hum of air conditioning broke the silence. He'd had a close call earlier—too close. Calloway's sharp glare and confrontational tone still rang in his ears. Ethan hadn't said much in response, but the manager's obvious annoyance meant he'd have to tread even more carefully. He couldn't risk raising any more suspicion. Not yet.

Ethan moved toward his locker, still dressed in his janitor's uniform, the fabric damp from hours of work. He reached for the lock and froze.

The door was slightly ajar.

His locker had been open.

A cold knot twisted in his stomach. No one else was supposed to touch it. He'd kept his personal belongings there—nothing critical, nothing that would outright expose him, but enough to make him uneasy.

He opened it fully, his pulse quickening. Everything seemed to be in place. His spare uniform was folded neatly on the top shelf, his water bottle sat where he'd left it, and his lunch container was still tucked in the corner. But then he noticed something out of place: his fake employee ID badge. It was lying flat on the bottom of the locker, out in the open. He was certain he'd put it in his pocket before starting his shift.

Ethan reached down and picked it up, examining it closely. There were no obvious signs that it had been tampered with, but the fact that it had been moved at all was enough to make his heart pound. Had someone been snooping? And if so, how much had they seen?

The locker room door creaked open, and Ethan tensed. He turned slowly, gripping the ID badge in his hand. Lena Ramirez stood in the doorway, her expression unreadable. She didn't look surprised to see him.

"You left your locker open," she said, her voice carefully neutral. "Thought you might want to know."

Ethan forced a smile, though his mind raced. "Thanks. Must've forgotten to lock it earlier."

Lena stepped inside, letting the door swing shut behind her. "You're lucky it wasn't someone else who noticed. Could've lost your stuff."

He nodded, slipping the ID badge into his pocket. "Good point. I'll be more careful next time."

She crossed her arms, leaning against a row of lockers. For a moment, she just looked at him. Her dark eyes seemed to study his every move, and Ethan felt an odd pressure building in the small room.

"You're a quiet one," she said after a long pause. "Always watching, always listening. Not like the other guys who just come in, do their thing, and leave."

Ethan shrugged, keeping his tone light. "Guess I'm just curious."

"Curious about what?" she pressed.

He hesitated. "About how things work around here. About the people who make this place run."

Lena's brow furrowed slightly. "That's not exactly typical janitor talk."

Ethan chuckled nervously. "Guess I'm not a typical janitor."

"No," she said softly, her gaze never leaving his face. "You're not."

The room seemed to shrink, the air heavy with unspoken questions. Ethan knew he had to redirect the conversation. If Lena suspected anything, if she was piecing together who he really was, everything could fall apart.

"I just… like to pay attention," he said. "Get a feel for the place. It's not every day you get to work in a building like this."

Lena didn't look convinced. She pushed off the lockers and took a slow step forward. "You know, I've been wondering something about you."

"What's that?" he asked, trying to keep his voice steady.

She tilted her head, studying him as if searching for a crack in his facade. "You know your way around here pretty well for someone who just started. You're always in the right place at the right time, always overhearing the most interesting conversations."

Ethan's grip on the locker door tightened. "I guess I've got a good sense of direction."

Lena's lips curved into a faint smile, but it wasn't one of amusement. "Maybe. Or maybe you're not who you say you are."

The room went silent. The hum of the air conditioning seemed louder, the shadows deeper. Ethan's heart pounded as he scrambled for a response. Denying it outright might only make her more suspicious, but admitting anything was out of the question.

"I'm just a guy trying to do his job," he said carefully. "Nothing more."

Lena took another step closer, her voice dropping. "People around here aren't stupid, Eli. They notice things. The way you talk, the way you carry yourself—it doesn't match your story. It's like you know things you shouldn't. And you're way too interested in how this company runs for a janitor."

Ethan swallowed hard. She was too smart for her own good. He had underestimated her, and now she was closing in on the truth.

"I'm just trying to keep my head down and do my work," he said, keeping his tone even. "If I seem curious, it's just because I like knowing how things work. That's all."

Lena didn't respond right away. She stood there, watching him with a mixture of suspicion and something else—something he couldn't quite identify. Then, slowly, she nodded.

"Sure," she said, though her tone suggested she wasn't convinced. "Just a janitor."

She turned and headed for the door, pausing with her hand on the handle. "But if you're hiding something, I'll find out. You can count on that."

Ethan stood frozen as the door swung shut behind her. His

mind raced, every nerve on edge. Lena was closer than anyone had come to figuring him out, and he couldn't afford another slip-up. If she found out who he really was, everything he was trying to do—the changes he wanted to make—could come crashing down before he had a chance to fix anything.

He turned back to his locker, carefully securing the lock this time. The night wasn't over yet, but it had already become clear that his disguise was beginning to crack. And as much as he wanted to believe he could keep the truth hidden, he knew deep down that the walls around his secret were getting thinner by the day.

Thirteen

The Big Reveal

The following day, Ethan found himself staring at his reflection in the restroom mirror, still in his janitor's uniform. The hum of the overhead lights was low, almost rhythmic, but it did nothing to calm his nerves. His mind was racing. He'd sensed it all night—the subtle change in how Lena looked at him, the pointed questions, the lingering stares. She knew something. Maybe she didn't have the full picture yet, but she was close enough to make him sweat.

He couldn't afford to slip up again, not after what had happened in the locker room. If she confronted him outright, he wasn't sure he could talk his way out of it. He'd played his part well until now, but the cracks were showing. She was sharp, and more importantly, she didn't trust easily. All it would take was one misstep, one wrong answer, and the entire facade would come crashing down.

As he dried his hands on a paper towel, the bathroom door opened behind him. Ethan caught a glimpse of Lena in the mirror, and his heart sank. She stood there, arms crossed, her expression carefully neutral but her eyes betraying a hint of something—determination, maybe? Curiosity? Whatever it was, it put him on edge.

"Eli," she said, her voice even. "Can we talk?"

Ethan turned, forcing a casual smile. "Sure. What's up?"

"Not here," she said, motioning toward the hallway. "Someplace quiet."

His stomach twisted. She knew. Or at least, she thought she did. The timing couldn't be worse. He had been planning to wait a little longer, to gather more information, to figure out the right way to approach her before coming clean. Now it seemed he wouldn't have that luxury.

Ethan followed her down the corridor, away from the noise of the call center. They stopped in a small, empty conference room, the glass walls fogged slightly from the night's humidity. Lena closed the door behind them and leaned against the table, arms still crossed.

She looked at him for a long moment before speaking. "You know, I've been thinking about something you said the other night."

Ethan kept his expression neutral, though his heart pounded

in his chest. "What's that?"

"You told me that people like me shouldn't have to put up with all this." Her gaze sharpened. "But that's not something someone in your position would normally say. Most people just keep their heads down and do their jobs. They don't ask questions. They don't try to understand what we go through."

"I'm just observant," Ethan said carefully. "Like I told you before."

Lena tilted her head. "It's more than that. You carry yourself differently. You talk like someone who knows a lot more than you let on."

Ethan's throat tightened. This was it. She was calling him out, and he had to decide how much of the truth to reveal—or how much longer he could keep pretending.

"I don't know what you mean," he said, keeping his voice calm. "I'm just here to do my job, like everyone else."

"Cut the crap, Eli," she snapped. "I know you're not who you say you are."

The words hit him like a punch to the gut. He opened his mouth, then closed it, struggling to find the right response. She took a step closer, her eyes narrowing.

"You think I haven't noticed how you seem to know exactly where everything is, how you always show up at just the right time, how you talk about the company like you've been here for years? You're not some regular guy off the street. So who are you really?"

Ethan's pulse thundered in his ears. He couldn't lie anymore—not convincingly, at least. But if he told her the truth, there was no going back. It wasn't just his cover that was at stake; it was the entire purpose of why he was here. If Lena found out he was Ethan Sinclair, the CEO she openly despised, he wasn't sure if she'd ever trust him again.

"I'm just—" he began, but she cut him off.

"Don't," she said, her voice cold. "I don't want another excuse or some half-baked story. I want the truth."

Ethan hesitated. The weight of the situation pressed down on him, suffocating. If he lied now, it might buy him time, but it would also destroy any chance of earning Lena's trust. And if he told her the truth, it could ruin everything. The entire plan. The entire reason he was here.

But looking into her eyes, he realized something. Lena didn't just deserve the truth. She needed it. She was one of the few people who still believed in doing what was right, even in a system that had repeatedly let her down. If he wanted any chance of fixing what was broken, he couldn't keep hiding behind a disguise.

"I'm not who I said I was," he admitted quietly, his voice barely above a whisper.

Lena's eyes widened, and for a moment, she looked almost triumphant. But then her expression hardened. "Who are you, then?"

Ethan exhaled, his hands curling into fists at his sides. "I'm Ethan Sinclair."

The words hung in the air between them, heavy and unrelenting. For a moment, Lena didn't react. She simply stared at him, as if processing what he'd just said.

And then, her expression shifted—shock, anger, betrayal all flashing across her face in rapid succession. She took a step back, shaking her head. "No. You're lying."

"I'm not," Ethan said, his voice steady now. "I'm the CEO of TitanTech. And I've been working here undercover to see what's really going on in my company."

Lena's laughter was bitter and sharp. "You expect me to believe that? You, the CEO of TitanTech, just decided to play janitor so you could… what? Spy on us?"

"It's not spying," Ethan said quickly. "It's—"

"It's deceit," she cut in, her voice rising. "You lied to me. To all of us."

"I needed to see what was really happening," Ethan said. "The reports I was getting weren't enough. I needed to understand the reality on the ground."

Lena shook her head again, her hands clenching into fists. "And you thought the best way to do that was to pretend to be one of us? To trick us into thinking you were just some guy trying to make a living? You think that makes it better?"

"It was never about tricking you," Ethan said, his voice filled with urgency. "It was about finding out what's wrong and fixing it."

She took another step back, her eyes narrowing. "You don't get it, do you? You don't just get to come down here, play the hero, and then waltz back to your penthouse once you've had your fun. You've been lying to me, to everyone, this whole time. And now you expect me to trust you?"

Ethan hesitated, the weight of her words crashing down on him. "I never wanted to hurt you," he said. "I never wanted to betray anyone. I just—"

"Stop," Lena said, her voice sharp and final. "You don't get to explain it away. You don't get to make this about your intentions."

She turned and stormed toward the door, her footsteps echoing in the quiet room. Just before she left, she glanced back at him, her expression filled with a mix of anger and disappointment. "You might be Ethan Sinclair, but you're no different than the rest of them."

The door slammed shut, leaving Ethan standing alone. The room was silent again, but this time it felt suffocating. He had known this moment would come, but he hadn't expected it to hurt this much.

Now, he had to face the fallout.

Fourteen

Damage Control

The conference room felt colder than usual, though Ethan knew it was just his nerves. He sat at the head of the long, glass table, his hands folded, his gaze fixed on the sleek digital clock on the wall. The rest of the room was empty—no bustling assistants, no board members, no one from the management team that he had trusted far too much.

No Lena.

The memory of her expression when she walked out last night still burned in his mind. The anger in her voice, the sharpness of her words—each one hit harder than he cared to admit. He had expected disappointment. He hadn't anticipated the depth of betrayal she must have felt. She wasn't just another employee to him. She had become the heart of what he wanted to protect, to fix. And he had let her down.

He couldn't just sit back and wait for her to come around, if she ever did. He had to act. The time for quiet observation was over. If he didn't step up, not just for Lena but for every employee whose voice had gone unheard, he would prove her right. That he was no different than the rest of them. That his promises of change were hollow.

Ethan pushed back his chair and stood. He had to start somewhere, and the place to begin was with the problem staring him in the face: Ryan Calloway.

He found Calloway in his office, leaning back in his chair, his feet up on the desk, scrolling through his phone. The man barely looked up as Ethan entered.

"Sinclair," Calloway said, the faintest smirk curling his lips. "Finally decided to come down from the penthouse and see how the little people live?"

Ethan ignored the jab. "We need to talk."

Calloway swung his legs down and sat forward, giving Ethan a mock-serious look. "Sure, boss. What's on your mind?"

Ethan stepped closer. He wasn't in the mood for games. "I've seen enough to know that the way you've been managing your team is completely unacceptable."

Calloway's smirk faltered, just for a second. He recovered quickly, leaning back again. "Unacceptable? I've been hitting every target you set. Meeting every quota. The numbers are good, Sinclair. Better than good."

"The numbers don't tell the whole story," Ethan said sharply. "Your team is burnt out. Morale is at rock bottom. People are afraid to speak up because they know you'll shut them down or threaten their jobs."

Calloway raised an eyebrow. "Afraid? You've been listening to too much gossip."

"Enough," Ethan snapped. "This isn't gossip. I've seen it myself. I went undercover, Calloway. I've watched how you run your department. I've seen the way you talk to people—Lena Ramirez, for one. Do you think I'm just going to let that slide?"

Calloway's expression darkened. He leaned forward, his elbows on the desk. "With all due respect, sir, you've been out of touch. You don't know what it takes to keep this place running. People need a firm hand."

"There's a difference between a firm hand and abuse," Ethan said, his voice steady. "You've crossed that line too many times. And as of now, you're done. Consider this your final warning. If I hear about one more incident—one more employee complaint—you're out. No severance. No recommendations. Do you understand me?"

Calloway opened his mouth to argue, but Ethan cut him off. "Do you understand?"

There was a long, tense silence. Calloway's jaw tightened, his gaze hard, but eventually, he nodded. "I understand."

Ethan turned on his heel and left, the door shutting behind him with a firm click. His heart was pounding, but he felt a surge of clarity. This was what he should have done from the start. This was the kind of action that Lena, and everyone else, deserved to see.

But his work was far from over.

Ethan spent the next several hours going through employee reports, performance reviews, and internal complaint files. He met with department leads, asked direct questions, and pushed past the usual corporate doublespeak. The deeper he dug, the more he realized just how widespread the problems were. Calloway wasn't the only issue. TitanTech's culture had been slowly poisoned by a system that valued short-term gains over long-term wellbeing. And it had happened on his watch.

He sent out an internal memo announcing an immediate review of all managerial practices, mandatory leadership training, and an anonymous feedback program for employees. It was a start— a small one—but he knew it wouldn't mean much unless he followed through.

And then there was Lena.

Ethan glanced at the clock again. It was late, but he couldn't wait until morning. He needed to talk to her, to explain why he had done what he did. He wasn't sure if she would listen, but he had to try.

He found her in the break room, a cup of coffee in her hands, staring out the window. The city lights stretched out in the distance, their glow reflected faintly in her tired eyes. She didn't look at him when he entered.

"Lena," he said quietly.

She didn't respond.

"I know I'm the last person you want to hear from right now," he continued. "But I need to say this."

She turned her head slightly, just enough to let him know she was listening. He stepped closer, keeping his voice steady.

"I lied to you," he said. "I lied to everyone. I thought going undercover was the best way to understand what was really happening here. I thought it would give me insight that I couldn't get from reports and meetings. But I realize now that I went about it the wrong way. I betrayed your trust, and I'm sorry."

Lena set her coffee down and turned to face him fully. Her expression was unreadable. "You think an apology is going to fix this?"

"No," Ethan said. "I know it's not that simple. I know I have a lot to prove before you can trust me again. But I'm not here to make excuses. I'm here to make it right."

Her eyes narrowed. "And how are you going to do that? Fire

Calloway and call it a day?"

Ethan shook his head. "It's bigger than Calloway. I've already started making changes, but I know it's just the beginning. I need to rebuild trust—yours, and everyone else's. And that's going to take time."

Lena crossed her arms, her gaze steady. "Why should I believe you'll follow through?"

"Because I have no choice," Ethan said. "If I don't fix this, I don't deserve to be in this position. I don't deserve the company I built. And I don't deserve the trust of people like you."

She studied him for a long moment. The silence stretched on, and Ethan felt every second of it. Finally, she let out a slow breath.

"You're right about one thing," she said. "It's going to take time. And actions speak louder than words."

Ethan nodded. "I'll show you. I promise."

Lena picked up her coffee again, her grip firm. "We'll see."

She turned back to the window, leaving Ethan standing there, his own reflection staring back at him in the glass. He had taken a step forward, but it was just the first of many. The road ahead was long, and trust wouldn't come easily.

But for the first time in a long while, he felt like he was moving in the right direction.

Fifteen

A Public Reckoning

Ethan stood in the empty boardroom, staring out over the glittering city below. The high-rise glass felt less like a privilege and more like a cage tonight, trapping him in the mess he'd allowed to fester. His own reflection stared back at him from the darkened window—haunted, tired, but determined. He wasn't the man he thought he'd been when he first founded TitanTech, and it had taken weeks of undercover work to reveal just how much he'd lost sight of his principles.

Tomorrow morning, that would change.

He turned and paced the room, his footfalls muted against the plush carpet. A single sheet of paper sat on the long, polished table—his notes for the all-hands meeting he had called. It wasn't something TitanTech did often. Usually, announcements came down from on high through sleek internal newsletters or filtered through department heads. A public reckoning, especially one led by the CEO, was unheard of.

Ethan knew the risk he was taking. If he mishandled this, it wouldn't just be his reputation at stake. Employees who were barely holding on would lose what little faith they still had. Investors might balk. The press, always eager for scandal, would pounce on any sign of weakness. But he also knew that if he didn't act now—if he didn't show everyone, especially people like Lena Ramirez, that he was willing to take responsibility— he would lose them all anyway.

He'd already sent out the invitations. Every employee at the company, from janitorial staff to senior engineers, had been informed of the meeting. He even extended the invitation to the interns who handled the smallest tasks. The entire workforce would either be in the building's central auditorium or tuning in via livestream. It was the only way to ensure the message reached everyone.

Now, standing alone in the quiet boardroom, Ethan closed his eyes and rehearsed the words he planned to say. He imagined the faces in the crowd—worn down, skeptical, maybe even angry. He imagined Lena sitting near the back, arms crossed, waiting for him to slip up. He imagined Ryan Calloway near the front, oozing faux confidence, no doubt convinced the CEO would protect him again. And he imagined the hundreds of others who hadn't spoken out, who had endured quietly, hoping for something better.

"I failed you," he murmured, testing the opening line. It felt honest. It felt right.

He paused, leaning forward on the table, his hands gripping the edge. For a moment, his resolve wavered. What if they didn't believe him? What if it wasn't enough?

No. He had to follow through. He owed them that much.

—-

The next morning, Ethan stepped onto the stage in the main auditorium. The space was packed. Employees filled the rows, their expressions a mix of curiosity, suspicion, and indifference. The glow of dozens of phone screens lit the audience as people live-tweeted, took notes, or simply scrolled to pass the time. Up on the stage, the lights were blinding. Ethan's chest felt tight, but he focused on the faces in front of him.

Lena was there, just as he'd imagined. She was seated near the middle, her arms crossed, her face impassive. Calloway, however, was conspicuously absent—something Ethan had expected. The man had been avoiding him ever since their last confrontation.

Ethan stepped up to the podium, adjusting the microphone. The room hushed as the last few murmurs faded away. The quiet was oppressive, the kind that made his throat dry and his palms slick with sweat. For a second, he gripped the edges of the podium to steady himself. Then he began.

"Good morning," he said, his voice carrying over the crowd.

"Thank you for being here."

He paused, scanning the room. There was no turning back now.

"I want to start with an apology," he said. "I failed you."

The room was silent. No one moved. Ethan pressed on.

"For too long, I've been disconnected from what goes on here. I built this company with the belief that it would be different— that we would innovate not just in technology, but in how we treat people. Somewhere along the way, I lost sight of that vision."

He glanced out over the audience. Some faces softened slightly, but many remained stone-faced. He couldn't blame them.

"Over the past few weeks, I've been taking a hard look at how things have been running here. I've seen the long hours, the burnout, the lack of support. I've seen how managers push you too hard, demand too much, and give too little in return. And I've seen how my own decisions—or lack of them—have allowed that to happen."

A faint murmur rippled through the crowd. Ethan held his ground, keeping his voice steady.

"I know some of you might be wondering why I'm only speaking up now. Why it took so long for me to acknowledge what you've been dealing with every day. The truth is, I wasn't paying attention. I trusted the systems I put in place, and I didn't look closely enough when things started to break down. That's on me. I take full responsibility."

The murmurs grew louder, a few heads nodding, a few skeptical glances exchanged. Ethan knew he wasn't winning them all over—not yet. But he was making progress.

"I've already started making changes," he continued. "We've implemented an anonymous feedback system so that everyone can report issues without fear of retaliation. We've begun reviewing every department's management structure, and we're prioritizing leadership training for all managers—starting at the top."

He let the words hang in the air for a moment before adding, "And that includes holding people accountable. I've spoken directly to managers who've been reported for abusive behavior. Some have been given warnings, others are facing disciplinary action. This is just the beginning."

At that, a few employees glanced at one another, whispering. Ethan took it as a sign to keep going.

"Most importantly, I want to hear from you," he said. "This can't be fixed by one person at the top. I need your voices, your experiences, your suggestions. My office—my actual office—is open to anyone who wants to talk. I'll be holding weekly office hours, and I promise you, I'll be there to listen."

A wave of quiet disbelief passed through the room. It was clear many didn't know whether to trust him. But that was expected. Trust wouldn't come overnight.

Ethan took a deep breath. "I know it's not enough to just say these things. I know I need to show you that I mean it. But I also want to thank those of you who've spoken up, who've fought to make this a better place even when it felt impossible. You've been the backbone of TitanTech, and you deserve to be treated as such."

He stepped back from the podium slightly, his hands gripping the edges once more. "We can do better," he said. "And we will."

The room was quiet for a moment, and then someone near the back started clapping. Slowly, others joined in. It wasn't thunderous applause, but it was something. A tentative show of acknowledgment. Ethan felt a flicker of hope.

As the meeting ended and employees began to file out, Ethan saw Lena lingering near her seat. She wasn't clapping, but she wasn't leaving either. Her arms were still crossed, her expression still guarded. But there was something in her eyes— something that looked a little less like anger and a little more like curiosity.

Ethan nodded to her as she finally turned to go. It was a small gesture, but it was enough. She didn't trust him yet, but maybe— just maybe—she was willing to watch and see what he did next.

Sixteen

A Grand Gesture

Ethan stood in the executive suite's darkened conference room, his hands braced against the cool, polished surface of the massive table. The room was eerily quiet, save for the faint hum of the building's ventilation system. Outside the floor-to-ceiling windows, the city stretched out like a field of glittering stars. Yet the grandeur of the view did little to calm him. His focus was elsewhere—on the folder that lay open before him, its pages filled with figures, project outlines, and a proposal that could either begin to right his company's many wrongs or backfire spectacularly.

He flipped through the documents one more time. His eyes scanned the rows of numbers, the proposed timeline, and the allocation of resources. Every detail had been carefully reviewed, every projection double-checked. But no amount of preparation could change the fact that what he was about to do was a gamble.

Ethan's thoughts shifted to Lena. She had been cold toward him since his revelation. Each interaction, no matter how brief, had felt like walking on broken glass. She didn't trust him—and why should she? He had lied to her, and to everyone else. The apology he offered at the all-hands meeting hadn't softened her stance. She'd stood at the back of the room, arms crossed, her face betraying neither anger nor approval. Just a guarded, skeptical stare.

He couldn't blame her. Words weren't enough. She needed to see action, to see real change. And that's exactly what Ethan intended to show her.

He closed the folder, tucked it under his arm, and headed out of the conference room. His footsteps echoed down the marble hallway as he made his way to his private office. The space was large and tastefully minimalist, with sleek furniture and abstract art adorning the walls. On the desk sat a single sheet of paper that carried a promise he intended to keep.

Ethan picked it up, reading it over one last time. The announcement of a new initiative, a complete overhaul of TitanTech's corporate culture, and a bold move to support employees at every level. The centerpiece of this plan was the nonprofit Lena had always talked about—a foundation that would provide resources, mentorship, and education for underprivileged communities. He had taken her words to heart, and now he was about to make her dream a reality.

The foundation wouldn't just be a token gesture. It would be backed by a significant portion of TitanTech's profits, ensuring that it had the funding to thrive. Ethan wanted it to be a lasting legacy—something that would outlive his tenure as CEO and benefit countless lives. It was a statement, a way of saying that TitanTech wasn't just about technology and innovation. It was about people.

He placed the announcement back on the desk and sat down, leaning back in his chair. The weight of his decision pressed down on him. He knew there would be resistance. Some board members would balk at the cost. Investors might see it as unnecessary philanthropy. But Ethan was done playing it safe. He had spent too long watching from the sidelines, allowing others to shape his company's culture. Now, he was taking control.

The next morning, Ethan arrived at the auditorium early. The room was set up for another company-wide meeting, but this one wasn't about apologies or promises. It was about action. Employees filtered in slowly at first, then in larger groups, filling the seats. Some carried coffee cups, others chatted quietly among themselves. Lena arrived just before the scheduled start time, slipping into a seat near the back. Ethan's heart gave a small, nervous flutter, but he pushed it aside. He had to stay focused.

As the room settled, Ethan stepped onto the stage. The lights were bright, but this time he didn't feel the same crushing pressure. He had a plan. He had something real to offer.

"Good morning," he began, his voice steady. "Thank you all for coming. I know it's only been a short time since our last meeting, but today isn't about apologies. It's about showing you that I mean what I say."

He paused, scanning the crowd. "Over the past few weeks, I've seen the challenges you face. I've seen how hard you work, how much you sacrifice, and how often your efforts go unnoticed. I've also seen the ways this company has failed you. And while words can acknowledge those failures, only actions can repair the damage."

Ethan reached into his jacket and pulled out the folder, holding it up. "This is the beginning of that action. Today, I'm proud to announce the launch of the TitanTech Foundation."

A ripple of murmurs spread through the audience. Some leaned forward, curious. Others exchanged skeptical glances. But Ethan kept going.

"The TitanTech Foundation will be a nonprofit organization dedicated to creating opportunities for those who need them most. We'll provide scholarships for underserved communities, mentorship programs for young talent, and resources for those who have been overlooked by the system. This isn't just a one-time donation or a PR move. This is a long-term commitment."

He paused, letting the words sink in. "And it's only possible because of you. Your hard work, your innovation, your dedication—this foundation is a reflection of the values that TitanTech should stand for. It's a way to give back, to ensure that we're not just building technology, but also building a better future."

The murmurs grew louder, but they were mixed with nods of approval. Ethan caught sight of Lena's face in the crowd. She was watching him closely, her expression still guarded, but her eyes held a flicker of something he hadn't seen before—interest, maybe even hope.

"This is just the first step," Ethan said. "I know there's more work to be done. I know that trust has to be earned. But I hope this shows you that I'm serious about making things right."

He closed the folder, tucking it under his arm again. "Thank you for listening. And thank you for your continued dedication. Together, we can build something truly extraordinary."

With that, he stepped off the stage. The applause was tentative at first, but it grew. Ethan didn't linger to bask in it. He left the stage and headed backstage, his mind racing with the next steps he needed to take. The foundation was just the beginning. He had to ensure it was implemented effectively, that it wasn't just a headline but a genuine force for change.

As the crowd began to disperse, Lena caught up with him in the hallway. She was still holding her coffee cup, and her expression was unreadable.

"Ethan," she said, stopping a few steps away.

He turned, bracing himself for whatever she might say.

"That… was unexpected," she admitted.

"Is that a good thing?" he asked cautiously.

She hesitated, then gave a small nod. "It's a start. But like you said, actions speak louder than words. We'll see."

Ethan felt a faint surge of relief. It wasn't forgiveness, but it was a step in the right direction. And for now, that was enough.

Seventeen

Lena's Choice

Lena sat in her tiny apartment's kitchen, staring at the notebook that lay open on the table. The pale yellow light of a single overhead bulb cast soft shadows over the cluttered surface—bills, her laptop, a half-empty mug of tea gone cold. Outside, the city hummed faintly, a constant background presence that she barely noticed anymore.

Her pen hovered over the page, motionless.

She had been here for nearly an hour, trying to write something, anything, to help her sort through the chaos in her mind. But every time she started, the words felt wrong. Too weak. Too unsure. So she'd scratched them out and tried again. Now the page was filled with smudged ink and crossed-out sentences, and she was no closer to figuring out what to do.

What to believe.

Ethan Sinclair. The name alone made her blood boil. For years, she'd thought of him as the unreachable figurehead of TitanTech—wealthy, untouchable, and indifferent to the struggles of the people who kept his company running. He was the man behind the machine, the one whose decisions trickled down and turned into impossible quotas, slashed budgets, and long, sleepless nights for employees like her.

Or so she had thought.

Now she wasn't sure.

The Ethan Sinclair she had met—Eli, she still thought of him as Eli sometimes—wasn't what she expected. He had lied to her, yes. He had pretended to be someone he wasn't, and that betrayal still stung. But when she looked past the initial anger, she saw something else.

He was trying.

That was the part she couldn't shake. He wasn't the aloof, callous CEO she had imagined. He had come down into the trenches, seen what she and her coworkers endured, and he was making changes. Real changes. The TitanTech Foundation wasn't just lip service—it was a genuine effort to give back. And his willingness to confront Ryan Calloway and push for accountability told her he wasn't afraid to challenge the toxic culture that had taken root in his company.

But could she trust him?

Lena pressed the pen to the paper again, her thoughts racing. Every instinct told her to keep her guard up. People like Ethan didn't just change overnight. He had spent years at the top, disconnected from the realities his employees faced. Could a few weeks undercover really transform him into someone who cared?

Her heart said maybe.

Her head said no.

She let out a frustrated sigh and set the pen down, rubbing her temples. She hated feeling like this—torn, uncertain, and vulnerable. For so long, she had relied on her own strength, her own determination. Trusting someone else, especially someone who had already lied to her, felt like giving up control.

And yet…

There was something in Ethan's eyes when he spoke to her. Something genuine. She had seen him stand up to Calloway, heard the passion in his voice when he talked about making things right. He wasn't just saying what she wanted to hear. He was putting himself on the line, risking his reputation, and potentially alienating his own board members to fix the mess he'd allowed to happen.

That kind of commitment wasn't easy to fake.

The notebook stared back at her, its crisscrossed lines and half-finished thoughts a reflection of the battle in her mind. She wanted to believe he could change. She wanted to believe he was sincere. But trust was a fragile thing, and she had learned the hard way how easily it could be shattered.

A soft knock at her apartment door broke her thoughts.

Lena frowned, glancing at the clock. It was late—too late for visitors. She rose from her chair and crossed the small living room, her bare feet soundless on the worn rug. Peering through the peephole, she felt a jolt of surprise.

It was him.

She opened the door a crack, her expression wary. "What are you doing here?"

Ethan stood in the hallway, his hands in his coat pockets. He looked tired, but there was something in his posture—something steady, unflinching.

"I need to talk to you," he said. "In person."

Lena hesitated. A part of her wanted to slam the door, to shut him out and keep her walls intact. But another part of her—a small, reluctant part—was curious. She stepped back and opened the door wider.

"Make it quick," she said.

Ethan stepped inside, his gaze briefly scanning the apartment before settling on her. "Thank you for letting me in."

"Just say what you need to say," Lena said, crossing her arms.

He nodded, then paused, as if choosing his words carefully. "I know I've hurt your trust. I know I've let you down, and I don't expect you to forgive me overnight. But I'm here because I want you to know that I'm serious about changing—about fixing what's broken."

Lena didn't respond right away. She watched him closely, searching for any sign of insincerity. "Why me?" she asked finally. "Why come to me?"

"Because you're the one who stood up when no one else would," Ethan said. "You're the one who fought for what was right, even when it was risky. I admire that. I respect that. And I want you to know that your voice matters."

Her heart twinged at his words, but she kept her expression neutral. "A lot of people have been saying that lately. That our voices matter. But what happens when the board pushes back? When the investors start complaining about the bottom line? What happens when it's not convenient for you anymore?"

Ethan met her gaze, his eyes steady. "Then I keep fighting. Because this isn't about convenience. It's about doing the right thing. I can't undo the mistakes I've made, but I can try to make sure they don't happen again."

Lena wanted to believe him. She wanted to trust that he was different, that he really did care. But trust was earned, not given.

"I don't know if I can believe you," she said, her voice soft but firm.

Ethan nodded, as if he'd expected that. "I understand. And I'll prove it to you—not with words, but with actions. All I ask is that you give me the chance to show you."

The room fell silent, the tension thick in the air. Lena felt her guard wavering, her walls starting to crack. She didn't know if she could fully trust him, but she also didn't know if she could shut him out completely.

"Fine," she said after a long pause. "I'll give you a chance. But only one. If you mess up again, we're done."

Ethan let out a breath he hadn't realized he was holding. "Thank you."

She stepped back, motioning toward the door. "You can leave now."

He nodded and walked to the door, pausing before he opened it. "Goodnight, Lena."

She didn't respond, her gaze fixed on the floor.

As the door clicked shut behind him, Lena leaned against the wall, her heart pounding. She didn't know if she had made the right choice, but she knew one thing: Ethan Sinclair wasn't going to give up easily. And maybe, just maybe, that was worth taking a chance on.

Eighteen

Love or Business?

Ethan stood in the hallway outside Lena's apartment, her words still echoing in his ears. The door had closed a moment ago, but the weight of the conversation lingered, heavy and uncertain. She'd given him a chance—one chance. It was more than he'd expected, but it wasn't without conditions. He knew how fragile that sliver of trust was, and he couldn't shake the feeling that it might shatter if he made even one wrong move.

For weeks, his mind had been consumed with fixing TitanTech, rooting out toxic management, and making the company a place where people like Lena could thrive. But as he walked down the dimly lit corridor, his thoughts kept circling back to her. She wasn't just an employee. She wasn't just a voice of reason or a symbol of the company's conscience. She was Lena. The woman who had challenged him, who had seen through his lies, and who, against all odds, had given him a chance to prove he was more than the man she thought she knew.

But was that chance about business—or something more?

Ethan sighed and stepped into the elevator, leaning against the cool metal wall. The past few months had been a whirlwind. Going undercover had changed everything he thought he understood about his company, his employees, and himself. It had forced him to confront the reality of his own failures, to admit that the image of himself as a forward-thinking, benevolent CEO was little more than a facade. But it had also led him to Lena, and that had made everything more complicated.

When he first met her, she was just another face in the sea of TitanTech employees. Another name in the complaint files. Another voice criticizing his leadership from a distance. But as he got to know her—really know her—he began to see the strength and passion that made her stand out. She cared deeply about her work, her colleagues, and the people around her. She wasn't afraid to speak her mind, even when it meant standing up to someone in power. And she had every reason to hate him. Yet she didn't walk away. Not entirely.

The elevator doors slid open, and Ethan stepped into the parking garage. His car was waiting, sleek and silent under the harsh fluorescent lights. As he climbed into the driver's seat, he stared at the steering wheel for a moment, his hands resting on the leather.

Love or business.

It wasn't a simple choice, but it felt like one.

His feelings for Lena weren't something he had planned. They had crept up on him slowly, catching him off guard. At first, it was just admiration—respect for her dedication and integrity. Then it was curiosity, a desire to understand what drove her. Before he knew it, he found himself looking forward to their conversations, to the moments when her walls came down and she allowed him to see the woman behind the fiery exterior.

But those feelings didn't erase the reality of the situation. He was still her boss—technically. He was still the CEO of a company that had let her down, and no amount of apologies or initiatives could change that. If he pursued her, if he allowed his personal feelings to cloud his judgment, it could jeopardize everything he was trying to fix. He couldn't afford to lose sight of the bigger picture.

Yet he couldn't ignore how he felt, either.

Ethan started the car, the engine purring quietly. As he drove through the empty streets, his mind raced. How could he separate what was best for the company from what was best for him? How could he make things right with Lena without letting his feelings complicate the already fragile trust between them?

By the time he reached his penthouse, the city had gone quiet. He stepped into the spacious living room, the floor-to-ceiling windows offering a breathtaking view of the skyline. But tonight, the view brought no comfort. He sank into the couch, staring out at the lights.

He could still see Lena's face, the way her expression had softened just slightly when she told him she'd give him a chance. It wasn't much, but it was something.

He knew what he had to do.

First, he needed to prove himself—not to Lena as a potential partner, but to Lena as a leader. He needed to show her that his promises weren't empty, that the changes he was making were real and lasting. He needed to ensure that TitanTech became the company she—and every other employee—deserved. Only then could he even consider pursuing something more personal.

The next morning, Ethan was at the office before sunrise. He spent hours in meetings with his executive team, outlining new policies and pushing for immediate action on the reforms he'd announced. He personally reviewed department budgets to ensure that the resources promised to overworked teams were actually being delivered. He met with employees from every level of the company, listening to their concerns, their ideas, and their frustrations.

He stayed late into the evening, poring over reports and drafting emails. But no matter how busy he was, Lena's words lingered in his mind. That chance she had given him wasn't just about the company. It was about proving he could be someone she respected, someone she could trust.

A week passed. Then two. Ethan threw himself into his work, determined to prove that he wasn't just another out-of-touch CEO. But no matter how much progress he made, he couldn't stop thinking about Lena.

One night, he found himself standing outside her apartment building again, the folder of updated foundation plans tucked under his arm. He wasn't sure if he should knock or walk away. Finally, he took a deep breath and pressed the buzzer.

When she opened the door, she looked surprised to see him. Her arms were crossed, her expression guarded, but she stepped aside and let him in.

Ethan held up the folder. "I wanted to show you something. It's the updated proposal for the foundation."

Lena took the folder, flipping through the pages. She didn't say anything right away, but her lips pressed into a thoughtful line.

"It's… better," she said finally. "Still a work in progress, but better."

Ethan nodded. "I'm committed to getting it right. And not just the foundation. Everything. I know I've made mistakes, but I'm doing everything I can to fix them."

Lena closed the folder and looked at him. "I'll believe it when I see it."

Her words stung, but Ethan didn't let it show. "You will," he said. "I promise."

She studied him for a long moment before setting the folder on the table. "Okay," she said quietly. "Let's see if you keep that promise."

Ethan left her apartment that night feeling more determined than ever. He had a long road ahead of him, but he was willing to do whatever it took—both for TitanTech and for Lena. Whether she would ever fully trust him again remained to be seen. But he wasn't giving up.

Nineteen

Tipping the Scales

Lena sat in the cramped back corner of the break room, her fingers loosely gripping a coffee mug that had long gone cold. The low hum of the vending machine filled the air as she stared at the tabletop, her mind turning over everything that had happened in the past weeks. The company-wide meeting, Ethan's sudden transparency, and the first tangible signs of change—it all seemed too good to be true.

She had seen Ethan moving through the building more frequently, talking to employees, sitting down in small conference rooms for what appeared to be informal check-ins. He no longer seemed like the distant, unreachable figure she had once imagined. Instead, he looked like someone who was trying— really trying. But for Lena, trust was still a fragile, tentative thing, and she had learned the hard way that promises meant little until they were backed by consistent action.

And then there was Ryan Calloway.

Lena had noticed the shift in him almost immediately after Ethan's all-hands meeting. Calloway's usual smirk was gone, replaced by a thinly veiled resentment that boiled just below the surface. He still walked through the customer service floor with his clipboard, but his steps seemed heavier, his words sharper. It was clear he felt the pressure of scrutiny bearing down on him.

But that pressure made him dangerous.

Lena's thoughts were interrupted when the break room door swung open. One of her coworkers, a young woman named Marisa, stepped in, her face pale and drawn. She clutched a piece of paper in her hand, and her eyes darted nervously around the room.

"Hey, Marisa," Lena said, sitting up straighter. "What's going on?"

Marisa hesitated, then crossed the room and sat down across from Lena. She placed the paper on the table, smoothing it out with trembling hands. "It's a warning," she said quietly. "Calloway sent it this morning."

Lena frowned and leaned in to read the paper. It was an official notice from HR, citing a performance issue that Marisa knew nothing about. Lena felt a flare of anger rise in her chest. "This is bullshit," she said, her voice low but firm. "You've been meeting your quotas all month."

Marisa nodded, her lips pressed tightly together. "I don't know what I did wrong. I thought I was doing everything right."

Lena sat back, her mind racing. She had seen this tactic before. When Calloway felt threatened, he doubled down on his control. He'd been reprimanded—if not directly, then indirectly—through Ethan's intervention. But instead of reflecting on his behavior, Calloway had taken it out on his team. Now he was targeting employees with fabricated issues to keep them in line.

She set the paper down and looked Marisa in the eye. "You're not alone in this," she said. "We'll figure it out."

Marisa gave a faint nod, but the fear in her eyes didn't disappear.

Lena left the break room feeling a simmering resolve building inside her. She couldn't just stand by and let this happen. She needed to act, but she needed to be careful. If she confronted Calloway directly, it would only make things worse. And if she went straight to Ethan… well, she wasn't sure she was ready to do that yet. She still didn't know if she could fully trust him.

But she also knew that staying silent wasn't an option.

Lena spent the rest of her shift quietly gathering information. She spoke to other employees, asking careful, non-threatening questions about their recent evaluations. The responses were consistent: out of nowhere, previously high-performing team members were receiving warnings or lower-than-expected performance scores. The pattern was undeniable. Calloway was retaliating against his team.

When her shift ended, Lena returned to her desk and stared at her screen. She opened her email, her fingers hovering over the keyboard. If she reported this directly to Ethan, it could put Calloway on the defensive—potentially triggering an even worse backlash. But if she didn't report it, Calloway would continue to intimidate and punish employees, and the cycle would never end.

Finally, she took a deep breath and began typing.

Subject: Concerns About Recent Performance Reviews

Ethan,

I wanted to bring something to your attention. Several employees in the customer service department have recently received performance warnings that don't align with their actual work. These are people who have consistently met or exceeded their quotas, yet they're being marked down for vague reasons.

I believe this is a direct result of the recent changes you've implemented. It seems that certain managers—specifically Ryan Calloway—are retaliating against their team members as a way to push back against your new policies.

I know you're working to improve the company's culture, and I appreciate the steps you've taken so far. But I felt it was important to let you know what's happening on the ground. This kind of behavior is exactly what needs to change.

Thank you for your time.
   Lena

She read the email over twice before hitting "Send." As soon as it was gone, a wave of nerves washed over her. Would Ethan act on it? Would he believe her?

The next day, Lena arrived at work to find Calloway in the middle of what appeared to be a performance review meeting with Marisa. He was speaking in a low, condescending tone, his arms crossed as he loomed over her desk. Marisa looked cornered, her shoulders hunched as she nodded along.

Lena clenched her fists at her sides, but she held back. This wasn't the time to jump in. She needed to wait and see if her email had made any impact.

Later that morning, a company-wide email appeared in everyone's inbox. The subject line was simple: "Clarification on Recent Policy Changes."

Lena opened it immediately. The message was from Ethan, and it outlined new safeguards for performance evaluations. All warnings and disciplinary actions would now require detailed documentation and third-party oversight. Employees could also appeal their evaluations through a newly established review board. It wasn't a perfect solution, but it was a clear step toward accountability.

Lena glanced across the room at Calloway. His jaw was set, his eyes narrowed as he read the email. For the first time, she saw uncertainty flicker across his face. He knew the rug was being pulled out from under him.

And then, to Lena's surprise, Ethan himself walked onto the floor. He made his way directly to Calloway's desk, stopping just short of standing over him. Lena couldn't hear their conversation, but she could see Calloway's body language shift. His usual bravado seemed to deflate under Ethan's steady gaze.

After a few tense minutes, Calloway got up from his chair and left the floor without a word. Ethan stayed behind, speaking with Marisa. Lena watched as her young coworker nodded, her expression slowly shifting from fear to relief.

When Ethan finally turned to leave, his eyes met Lena's. She held his gaze, her expression guarded, but something had changed. She still wasn't sure if she could fully trust him, but for the first time, she felt a sliver of hope.

Maybe Ethan Sinclair wasn't just talking. Maybe he really was tipping the scales.

Twenty

Boardroom

Ethan paced the length of the conference room, his hands buried deep in the pockets of his suit trousers. The sunlight streamed through the floor-to-ceiling windows, casting long shadows on the polished table and sleek leather chairs. He'd never been a man prone to second-guessing, but today was different. Today, he was walking into a meeting that would define his company's future and his own.

The board had been growing restless. For weeks, they'd tolerated his newfound push for accountability, his promises to change the company culture, and his public show of humility. But now, the cracks in their patience were showing. Some directors had whispered concerns about the Titan Tech Foundation's potential impact on their bottom line. Others had questioned his decision to reshuffle senior management. A few, he suspected, saw his new initiatives as an unnecessary risk in a company that had always prided itself on steady growth.

He stopped pacing and turned to face the door just as the first members began to arrive.

The first was Charlotte Monroe, an older woman with sharp features and an even sharper tongue. She'd been on the board longer than Ethan had been CEO and never missed an opportunity to remind him of that fact.

"Good morning, Ethan," Charlotte said, her tone cordial but distant. "I trust you've prepared a thorough explanation for your recent… ventures."

"I have," Ethan said evenly. "We'll go over everything."

Next came Marcus Bell, a younger, ambitious director who always seemed one step away from staging a coup. He nodded curtly, his expression unreadable, as he took his seat.

One by one, the others filed in, their movements deliberate, their faces composed. They made polite conversation about the weather, the latest stock market shifts, and their weekend plans. But underneath the pleasantries, Ethan could feel the tension building.

Once everyone was seated, Ethan moved to the head of the table. He glanced around at the faces of the people he'd once thought of as allies. Now, he wasn't so sure.

"Thank you all for being here," he began, his voice steady. "I know there's been a lot of discussion recently about the changes I've implemented. Today, I want to address those concerns head-on."

Charlotte leaned back in her chair, her fingers steepled. "We appreciate the opportunity, Ethan. But let's not waste time. You've made some very public moves—moves that have raised questions among our investors. They're not used to seeing TitanTech engage in what they perceive as… charitable endeavors."

"It's more than charity," Ethan said, meeting her gaze directly. "The TitanTech Foundation isn't just a philanthropic effort. It's an investment in the future of our workforce, our innovation pipeline, and our reputation. By supporting underserved communities, we're building a stronger, more diverse talent pool. And by improving our internal culture, we're ensuring that the best and brightest want to work here—and stay here."

"Be that as it may," Marcus cut in, "we've already seen a dip in our quarterly earnings projections. Investors are nervous. They want to know that we're still focused on growth."

Ethan nodded. He had expected this. "I understand their concerns. That's why I've prepared a detailed plan that outlines how these initiatives will not only improve our culture, but also drive long-term profitability. Better employee retention means lower recruitment costs. A more inclusive workforce means broader market insights. And the goodwill generated by the foundation positions us as a leader not just in technology, but in corporate responsibility."

A few board members exchanged glances. Charlotte's lips tightened into a thin line.

"Ethan," she said, her tone measured, "we've all supported you through difficult decisions before. But this is uncharted territory. TitanTech has always been known for its stability and measured growth. This new direction feels… reckless. Investors thrive on predictability, and right now, they're not seeing it."

"It's true," said another board member, James Aldridge, who rarely spoke but carried significant weight when he did. "We've all seen the reports. Investors are worried about their dividends, and some are questioning your leadership."

Ethan felt the sting of James's words, but he refused to waver. "I understand their concerns, and I'm not asking for blind trust. I'm asking for the chance to prove that this path—while different—will yield results. I've already started seeing the impact internally. Employee feedback is improving. Turnover rates are slowing. These are the first steps toward a stronger, more resilient TitanTech."

The room was silent for a moment. Then Charlotte leaned forward, her voice colder than before. "We don't run a charity, Ethan. We run a business. And if the shareholders start losing confidence in you, it's our responsibility to act."

Ethan straightened his posture, his jaw tightening. "I'm well aware of that, Charlotte. But I'd argue that maintaining a company culture where employees feel valued, where our reputation as an ethical leader sets us apart, is just as critical as quarterly profits. In fact, it's the foundation for long-term success."

Marcus leaned in, his tone skeptical. "And if the investors disagree?"

Ethan's gaze swept across the table. "Then I'll answer their questions directly. I'll show them the data, the projections, and the long-term benefits. I'm not hiding behind promises. I'm backing this with actionable steps and measurable outcomes."

The room fell silent again. The board members glanced at one another, their faces betraying no clear consensus.

Finally, Charlotte sighed. "We'll review your plan in detail. But know this, Ethan—our patience isn't unlimited. If you can't deliver the results you're promising, we'll have to reconsider our leadership."

Ethan met her gaze evenly. "Understood. But I believe in what we're doing, and I'll prove that it's the right choice."

The meeting adjourned shortly after, the board members leaving the conference room in quiet clusters. Ethan remained at the table, staring at the now-empty seats. The weight of their skepticism was heavy, but he had expected this fight.

As the door clicked shut behind the last director, Ethan leaned back in his chair. He had always known that change wouldn't come easy, but he hadn't anticipated just how much resistance he would face from his own board. Still, he refused to back down.

He thought of Lena—her determination, her willingness to stand up for what was right, even when it was risky. If she could fight for a better future, so could he. Ethan knew the path he had chosen was steep and fraught with obstacles, but he was prepared to climb it.

Because this wasn't just about saving TitanTech's reputation. It was about saving its soul.